Die Laughing
War Humour from
WW1 to the Present Day

George Korankye

First edition
Published in Great Britain
By Mirage Publishing 2008

Text Copyright © George Korankye 2008

First published in paperback 2008

A CIP catalogue record for this book
Is available from the British Library.

ISBN: 978-1-90257-844-6

Mirage Publishing
PO Box 161
Gateshead
NE8 4WW
Great Britain

Printed and bound in Great Britain by

Book Printing UK
Remus House, Coltsfoot Drive, Woodston, Peterborough, PE2 9JX

Cover © Mirage Publishing
Layout by Artistic Director Sharon Anderson

Papers used in the production of this book are recycled,
thus reducing environmental depletion.

On 10 July 2008, Cathy Gibson died suddenly. Cathy was a dear friend, she was like a mother to me. She was funny, witty and could come up with sayings that would have you roaring with laughter. After a hip replacement, she walked with the aid of a stick. This stick became her threatening 'weapon of mass prodding' to coerce any individual who did not do her bidding.

Her death made me realise the pain and suffering that must have accompanied the passing away of countless dear loved ones in wartime.

Writing this book, therefore, is a poignant reminder to everyone to think of the tragic deaths war has brought in its wake. Our loved ones maybe 'here today and gone tomorrow', but they are not forgotten.

Have we really learned the lessons from the past that resulted in the countless deaths because of war?

'What we do in life, echoes in eternity'
North American Indian

V

Acknowledgements

I would like to thank Random House Publishing, especially Gabrielle White for all her help and also for waiving their copyright fees. She also pointed me to WATCH (Writers, Artists and their Copyright Holders) to ensure that I would not fall foul of any copyright violations. My thanks too to David Sutton of Reading University, UK director of WATCH for advice.

My appreciation also goes to Shiel Land Associates for permission to use materials from Miles Noonan. I am indebted to *The Sunday Post*, *Express Newspapers*, *The Times*, National Archives, Imperial War Museum and the various media who provided me with materials and at times waiving their royalty fees.

However all this would not be possible if it were not for Steve, Johnny and Sharon at Mirage Publishing. At times I tried their patience with my lack of computer publishing skills. What publisher will phone a novice writer personally to give them helpful counsel? Well, Steve did! Thanks!

Also to my rescue came my new son-in-law Graeme to help with my lack of computer skills.

Thanks Stephan for the photos and you too Jordon for the cartoons of the various stories. I hope you get some work because of this book.

Last but not least, thanks to my mum for the financial support and Sharon my dear wife for putting up with a messed up living room. Sorry for all the strewn books, magazines, letters and other paraphernalia that messed up your living room for months, especially as publishing deadline approached.

Contents

Preface

'If you see no reason for giving thanks,
the fault lies in yourself'
                                    Minquass Indians of America

Countless people have asked what on earth made me undertake such a mammoth project. Could my time not have been used more productively, such as counting how many people I see using their mobile phones while driving or even estimating how many sheep I pass on my way to work? A bit woolly, eh? Please allow me to sheepishly explain: sorry to bleat on. In fact, if you are reading this book now, you have no option but to keep on reading for an answer, as I am sure I have your undivided attention.

My original plan was to pull together accounts relating to wartime humour covering the First World War to the current troubles in Iraq with materials solicited from the public. The response has been tremendous, in fact magnanimous, to the extent that I had to curtail my material drastically and commence a second volume - look out for it (look upon this as Vol. 1).

The initial idea came to me while I was working as a Radiographer in Scotland. I would deal with patients (and their relatives) of all ages, sexes, races, professions and cultures: from newborn babies to geriatrics whom, sadly, were very close to the grave.

In fact, Shakespeare was right when he said 'twice a babe, once a man'. We are born into the world as helpless, weak infants, and at times end our lives as

9

vulnerable, frail adults, unable to speak coherently, or do even the simplest tasks.

I came across all kinds of situations in my job. Several were attempted suicides, quite a few road traffic accidents and many, of course, the victims of assaults by 'nutters', both male and female, who 'tool' themselves with knives and all manner of implements to inflict the maximum pain and suffering on individuals who just happen to be at the wrong place at the wrong time. Robert Burns (1759-1796) was quite right when he said 'man's inhumanity to man make countless thousands mourn'.

Any Radiographer, in fact any health professional, will tell you that they will see and deal with more traumatic situations in a few years than most people encounter in a lifetime. Death and suffering become a routine part of the job.

I noticed the grief that accompanied illnesses and accidents, some due to unforeseen circumstances while others were self inflicted.

I could not also fail to be touched by the devotion of mothers as they sat with their premature babies, talking and cuddling them.

Scenes of that nature always brought to my mind the poem by the famous children's poet Ann Taylor (1782-1866):

Who ran to help when I fell,
And would some pretty story tell,
Or kiss the place to make it well?
My mother.

Not to be forgotten are the children with sad, tearful eyes who watch their parent's life slowly ebbing away.

Then there are the casualties of heartless criminals who pound, kick, knife and punch their victims mercilessly until they are either unconscious or unable to offer any worthwhile resistance, now spread serenely on a hospital trolley, senseless and beaten to a pulp.

Other victims take their punishing or pasting with less resistance, but certainly not mutely. They arrive in a crescendo of sounds: police and ambulance sirens, screams of anguish from worried parents mixed with their own pitiful cries of pain and bewilderment.

The ignoble sight of someone's son, daughter, mother or father would make you assume that this human, without any professional boxing skills or know-how, had involuntarily gone ten rounds with Mike Tyson. Some patients would win an Oscar for makeup with their trampled swollen faces, protruding lips and blackened puffy eyes.

I would often wish that if only some of these judges could come to the 'chalk face' see for themselves what we in the medical profession, the police and all the other heath professionals and ancillary workers, have to deal with, all over the UK, on a regular basis, picking up the pieces of 'civilian war casualties'. Some hospitals can resemble a war zone at times. It truly is a jungle out there. In fact, we talk of humans behaving indistinguishably from animals; this view is an insult to animals, as they would not treat other creatures of their own kind the way some of us behave towards each other.

Am I depressing you?

However, there is another, thankfully positive and admirable, side of human nature which is shown time and time again, which makes you realise that, yes, the world is indeed uncaring at times but some also show compassion and are not there just to make a wage.

11

Preface

Consider the nurses in the intensive care units, who talk softly in low monotones to unconscious patients, confident they can be heard in their quiet world, with all sorts of drips going into every orifice amid the sounds of constant bleeping machines with their hypnotic electronic sounds. To be in such a situation and not be moved emotionally would be hard-hearted indeed.

The challenge, therefore, was not to bring the occupation home, but to be able to divorce myself from such episodes. I will be honest and say it was at times very, very difficult!

I always tried to bring a touch of humour to those whose lives my paths had inadvertently crossed. I found that a witty saying, a humorous joke or words at the right time would lift a person's spirits.

In one case, a poor wee old lady was looking rather dejected. After x-raying her, I kneeled in front of her wheelchair and, passing my open hand across her eyes, asked her, 'What kind of milk is this?' She looked puzzled. I then replied, 'Past your eyes (Pasteurised).' Get it? Well, it is worth all the money in the world to see a dejected person suddenly smile. No, it may not be a hearty laugh but, boy, does it bring a ray of sunshine to that person's life and, of course, mine too.

This started me ruminating. Using my knowledge gained at Queen Margaret University, I started to mentally make notes and noticed that it seemed to appear that patients who laughed, accepted their predicament with a quiet dignity, were happier than those who adopted a 'Why me?' attitude.

Those with the latter approach were more difficult to deal with; in addition, they were usually very negative in their outlook. No amount of kind words or humour could lift their spirits.

Die Laughing - George Korankye

Yes, it soon became crystal clear that laughter made people who were facing traumatic situations relax more and become more contented. It certainly lifted their spirits as well as mine.

So the next time you are in a hospital setting, either as a patient or visitor, in fact the next time ANYONE, ANYWHERE does something for you, let it be your normal reflex action to thank them. Philosopher Meister Eckhart (1260-1328) provides words that perhaps we all can bear in mind. His advice is: 'If the only prayer you said in your whole life was "thank you", that would suffice'.

Most historians accept that World War I was indeed a watershed in man's history. To develop this theme and to establish whether there was a market for a publication about wartime humour, I contacted newspaper editors asking if they could appeal to their readers for humorous stories, satires, anecdotes, etc, covering all walks of life during war years. I also began trawling various publications printed in the past, and websites to see if I could supplement readers' responses. My appeal to the various editors was successful. Enough real life stories were received and collated to enable me to write two volumes. In fact, even while I am writing this current edition, material is still coming in![1]

The media attention has been tremendous and for this I cannot help but express my profound and sincere gratitude to all newspaper editors who granted me my

---

[1] By way of example, from Eire comes courtesy of Shaun O'Byrne the following: '…For my part I enclose cartoons that is one of two found in an autograph book belonging to my great grandaunt "Bridget Anne O'Byrne", schoolmistress. Both drawings are by Thomas Shiels. Various romantic verses suggest he was an admirer of hers. I can only guess if he was a soldier and this is a self portrait.'

requests and, of course, to all those who responded generously by donating precious scrapbooks, old cartoons books, poems, nostalgic postcards and letters of their loved ones, some of whom are no longer with us. In fact, some of the materials received predate 1914.

Readers pointed me to various publications with the result that some of the materials complement readers' replies. <u>Sadly this has resulted in some of the public's support being excluded in this publication</u>.

If this publication is successful, it certainly will not be due to my writing skills alone, but also attributable to the generous donations of you, the public. To all who helped me in such a generous way, I want to say A BIG THANK YOU.[2]

---

[2] A careful appraisal of the footnotes and bibliography section will bear testimony to the input others have given me in the compilation of this work, some going as far as waiving payment of royalties.

An old Malayan proverb says: 'One can pay back a loan of gold, but one dies forever in debt to those who are kind'. Mark Twain also said: 'Kindness is the language which the deaf can hear and the blind can see'.

I realise that you ALL, in all probability, had other matters that took up your precious time, but the fact that you considered my requests for information and in addition will go out to buy this compilation of experiences is indeed greatly appreciated.

So once again, a BIG THANK YOU (repetition for emphasis). 'The smallest act of kindness is worth more than the grandest intentions', as Oscar Wilde famously said.

Whatever sex you are, whatever colour, creed or nationality, if you sent me any information then I want you to feel that I thoroughly value your help extended to me. As Einstein said, 'Try not to be a man (or woman) of success but rather try to be a man (or woman) of value'.

This fact is worthy of reiterating, as without help from others this collection of incidents would not have been successful. Therefore, I want you all to reflect on the words of Isaac Newton (1643-1727): 'If I have seen farther than others, it is because I have stood on the shoulders of giants'.[3]

You may not feel comparable to giants, but your little 'pygmy' assistance made it possible to complete this huge assignment in a very short space of time and to me, therefore, you are all gigantic as far as I am concerned.

By the way, if anyone wants to send in stories for the next volume, please e-mail them to

---

[3] I have also benefited from 'academic' giants whose historical writings are second to none. Works by Max Arthur, Richard Holmes and Lyn McDonald are examples. Many more are cited in the reference section.

warhumour@btinternet.com[4] or contact my publisher at Mirage Publishing.[5] I hope you enjoy reading these events with the same pleasure I had in writing and compiling them.

Let me give you a foretaste of what awaits you. Norman Burgess, speaking about his mother Winifred, relates: 'My mother was in the WVS (Women's Voluntary Service) for all of the war and spent some time in the blitzed areas of London in a canteen. However, this story occurred nearer home. She was issuing earplugs early on in the war, and had gone up one road and half way down another, when an elderly gentleman said plaintively, "I do have two ears, you know". You can guess what she had been doing.'

By the way, before anyone writes to the various newspapers and says, 'I knew so and so and I know exactly what happened…he/she has been economical with the truth…', mull over these questions: What was in it for them? Nothing! Why? Firstly, no monies were exchanged for any contributions. This means there was no pecuniary advantage for anyone. Secondly, no guarantees were given that items sent in would be automatically included in the book in order to preserve the memories of dear loved ones for nostalgic, historical or for the benefit of future generations. In short, there was nothing in it for donors, and no media attention was assured.

That leaves only one conclusion, which is that individuals, out of the goodness of their hearts, decided to help me. For example, Ian Anderson of Cheshire wrote in after sending me information:

---

[4] Please would anyone who reads this book also send their comments to me. Thanks! **warhumour@btinternet.com**

[5] See last page of book jacket for contact details.

'A look around the history of World War I books in Cheshire Libraries has not produced anything...I shall keep my eyes open for anything else that may be helpful. Good luck to your writing.'

In the light of his comment, which, by the way, permeates all correspondences received, let me ask you: What were the contributors' motives? Altruism, pure and simple! Imagine someone trawling through books at a library in their own time in order to help a complete stranger.

Is that not self sacrificing to an extreme degree? If that is the case, then surely it behoves us to give them the benefit of doubt. Please apply the proverb of the Omaha Indians of America: 'Respect the gift and the giver'.

To conclude, can I ask you all a favour? Firstly, please do not be quick to condemn the quality of some of the images. A considerable number of them are old, and I mean really old, like 1914 and beyond.

Taking into account storage as well as time and other environmental factors - there is no way, even with the best of scanning technology today, to reproduce them and present them in their original condition.

Secondly, look upon the stories as truthful accounts by individuals sent in good faith. Time may have affected certain memories and recollections, but please 'chew over' the spirit in which the articles were contributed.

It is very unlikely that individuals would set out deliberately to fabricate, embellish or deceive with their stories.

Thirdly, don't be quick to run to lawyers to inform them that I have breached someone's copyright. I have contacted WATCH (Writers, Artists and Their Copyright Holders). This is '...a database of copyright contacts for writers, artists, and prominent figures in other creative fields.

WATCH [6] is run jointly by the Harry Ransom Centre and University of Reading Library.' I have therefore demonstrated 'good faith' and have done all that is reasonable possible to find the copyright holders, get their permission(s) and pay any royalties rightly due to them. Where readers have sent in images from scrapbooks, etc, consent has been given for reproduction.

It is therefore the responsibility of every reader who picks up this book to read it in a trusting manner and not to 'nit pick' by severely criticising every detail, looking for loopholes, mistakes, etc. Just enjoy the book, have a good laugh and, who knows, 'YOU MAY ACTUALLY DIE LAUGHING!'

---

[6] www.watch-file.com

Introduction

'To jaw-jaw is always better than to war-war'
Sir Winston Leonard Spencer Churchill (1874–1965)

It must be stated at the outset that this is not a book on either the history of war or the history of humour. It is also not a compilation of experiences without comment. Other authors, for example Max Arthur, have covered this topic – see bibliography section.

Therefore, please bear in mind that, although not a historical book, it is historically accurate. It does not follow war in a chronological manner. The reason is that the effects of war do not change. The book is therefore intended to show the aspects of humour during times of war-adversity. However, whenever historic events are referred to, this is accurate. Full lists of referenced materials are listed in the bibliography section.

The book commences in this section with a brief overview or synopsis of the results of war. Subsequent topics cover the universality of humour, its benefits and how this aspect of human nature is used world wide to cushion adversity. It develops this theme throughout the chapters. Iconic images such as Kitchener's 'Your country needs you' is discussed under the title 'The Enduring power of an image'. A chapter informs the reader about the uniqueness of the pivotal date of 1914.

Additional sections cover the armed forces, the role of women, the home front and blackouts, war's legacy, the forgotten 'army' such as the Bevin Boys, and train drivers, remembrance and the future.

Introduction

In all the chapters, images, poems, satires, 'pithy' sayings and anecdotes sent in by ordinary people are featured; some of these are historic, others current. A few members of the public pointed me to other publications and websites, such as the BBC's *WW2 The People's War*[7], which are quoted and referenced where necessary. In fact, one reply was from a member of parliament, sadly his contribution could not be included, such are the variety of responses and materials from individuals who responded.

Stories from all walks of life, social classes and professions, from all corners of the UK, including Northern Ireland, the Channel Islands, the Isle of Wight, Eire (Southern Ireland) and even a poem from Canada by an ex prisoner of war who was incarcerated in Stalg 3 are featured.

A number of images and poems dating from 1914 onwards are featured. These have been scanned and incorporated in the book to give the reader a real feel of authenticity. You can actually laugh with people you have never known. Genuine stories of the hilarity of people facing adversity or who were about to die will touch your hearts. Let me give you a sample of this.

RAF Flying Officer Ken Adams of 609 Squadron in 1944 relates a rather sad story he tells of his comrade, Canadian pilot Piwi Williams,[8] when he was shot down, his plane descending in flames to the ground. He knew the end was nigh. In a few moments he would be gone –

---

7 WW2 People's War is an online archive of wartime memories contributed by members of the public and gathered by the BBC. The archive can be found at www.bbc.co.uk/ww2peopleswar.

8 *Lest We Forget: Forgotten Voices from 1914-1945* by Max Arthur (2007) p202. Courtesy Random House Publishing.

dead - yet he managed in his dying moments to radio his colleague. Ken Adams in recounting the story says: '…he called back and said that he was hit and paralysed, and he went slowly down for several minutes. I will never forget his last words, just before he hit the ground: "Order me a late tea".'

Do those words not touch your heart? It certainly touched Ken Adams' heart. Why? Because if any of us were facing our last moments, what would be our main concern? Would it be saying a final prayer of repentance to a deity, or perhaps a message on the radio to be relayed to our wife, children and loved ones of our undying love for them? Some may even add that they hope to see them in the 'next world'.

The point is, we will all probably have last wishes or sayings. Certainly the last thing on our minds would be telling the one who was to relay this last message to inform our loved ones we would be late for tea. That is the kind of humour that this book is tainted with. In addition, you will read first hand the stories of women and the struggles they had to cope with while in a workplace which was previously dominated by men.

This is not a political book, nor is it intended to argue the pros and cons of war. At times statistics are quoted but it is with the sole purpose of helping the 'younger' reader and those who have never experienced such conditions to get a feeling of the magnitude of casualties, or to drive the point home of the sufferings being inflicted and steadfastly endured by the whole nation. Each statistic is a human with an extended family. A casualty of war, be it by death or injury - physically, emotionally or psychologically - can resemble a pebble being dropped in a lake, the ripples slowly radiating outward. The effect of one action on an individual has a ripple effect on other people's lives and, at times, on a country's future policies.

In writing this book, one theme seems to run through all the stories: the tremendous sufferings that war brings to ALL, whether 'combatants or aggressors'. Over 90 decades later, scores of people remain haunted by terrible memories.

Although I have tried to find humorous incidents, this book is not intended to trivialise the appalling miseries inflicted on humans because of war.

A fitting symbol that the world should embrace is the statue that graces the United Nations building. It is a sculpture that is iconic, easily recognisable; its pithy message taken from the Bible is that mankind desperately needs a release from the burdens that warfare imposes by channelling his energies from developing weapons of destruction to producing weapons of 'peaceful' construction.

Compared to a sword, what possible damage can a plough used for tilling land do to a human being? A blade has a dual purpose, its function is either peaceful or violent, whereas a plough's application is non-aggressive.

Can you recollect when you last heard of someone being sadistically killed by a plough? Whether Christian, Pagan, Jewish, Moslem, Hindu, Zoroastrian, Buddhist, in fact whether you believe in a God or not, or consider yourself to be a Humanist, you surely must agree that war imposes incredible emotional, financial, physical and psychological costs? However, the greatest price is the millions upon millions of lives lost.

After a major conflict, ships that disappeared to watery graves beneath the sea lie as silent testimony to the carnage that took place above on the earth.

Aeroplanes downed or shattered in the air, some of which join 'shipmates' in the realms below, taking cargoes of dead or dying souls with them. Yes, these ships as well as planes can be replaced by bigger, better versions.

Architects rebuild the destroyed houses, fill in bomb-crated holes, ironically with debris from buildings that had caved in, now beyond repair, or had to be demolished because of explosions caused by the ordnances dropped from the skies. Flower beds, lush green grass, new housing blended into a re-landscaped earth can thus go a long way in erasing the physical destructive forces left by the military.

Within a few decades, there is hardly any physical evidence of the carnage caused, except of course for the mines laid, the unexploded shells fired in anger, the bombs whose timing devices failed to activate. These devices can still claim fatalities long after the end of the war.

To a lesser extent, we can achieve comparable results for sufferers. Psychologists can help with the rehabilitation of the thousands of confused minds. Engineers operating in conjunction with surgeons, once again using the appliance of science, can reshape millions of artificial limbs using prosthetics with better sophisticated manoeuvrability which, while not equal to an original arm or leg that had to be amputated or was severely broken, can still restore a fair bit of movement to a devastated body part.

Unknown too, we must not forget, are those who never fully recover. Sitting in homes, numerous individuals experience, over and over again, their ordeals, not missing out any gory details. Unreported are those, either too proud to ask for help, or not wishing to burden the country they gave up comfortable normal existences for. They go to beds only to wake up with cold sweats as they relive nightmares night after night, day after day, week after week, month after month, year after year, decade after decade.

They fail to grasp the help extended to them by charities or government agencies. Resembling the ships they served in that are submerged at the bottom of the sea, or the planes that they flew in which came crashing to the ground, they wait silently in 'limbo', as they slowly begin to deteriorate. Thousands, perhaps millions, unrecorded souls take confused, damaged minds to graves.

Others retain the physical effects of war in their bodies by a lethal killer called 'shrapnel', an assassin that cannot be removed by the skill of any surgeon. It waits silently in the body, biding its time when it will move with more dexterity than a snake and strike a fatal blow by blocking a blood vessel (thrombosis) or causing massive swellings in a vein or artery (aneurysm) and which eventually bleeds in the mind or anywhere in the person's anatomy where it has made its home. This killer is deadlier than any 'agent provocateur', more treacherous than a spy, as insidious as some known cancers.

These individuals carry the effects of war, not in their minds but in their bodies. For them also the war will never ever finish, as every day lived is a bonus.

Certainly, long after its conclusion every war leaves a deadly silent legacy in its wake; a 'present' which the enemy has unwittingly or knowingly bestowed upon them, a gift they would rather not have and would gladly exclaim 'Thanks, but no thanks!'

With his accumulated reservoir of scientific knowledge and understanding of cryogenics, DNA manipulations that has caused so much debate, man cannot currently bring back the greatest casualty: the millions dead, those that never returned to loved ones, who forfeited that precious commodity of life and who now lie in such places as Flanders fields.

In view of all the effects associated with any argument that gradually escalates into a fight between two nations, would you say that it is not foolish to ask this million dollar question: 'Will man ever be able to fulfil the UN's dream of a peaceful earth?'[9] Or are we for eternity going to say what Aristotle, the Greek Philosopher (384-322BC), once said: 'We make war that we may live in peace'? Only time will tell.

---

[9] The bronze sculpture 'Let Us Beat Our Swords into Ploughshares', was created by Soviet artist Evgeny Vuchetich, and presented to the United Nations on 4 December 1959 by the Government of the USSR. The sculpture, depicting the figure of a man holding a hammer aloft in one hand and a sword in the other, which he is making into a ploughshare, is meant to symbolise man's desire to put an end to war, and to convert the means of destruction into creative tools for the benefit of mankind. It is located in the North Garden of the United Nations Headquarters. ©UN Images.

Chapter 1

Universal Humour and its Benefits

'When you drink the water, think of the well-digger'
                                            Russian proverb

Would you not agree that humour is woven into human nature? It courses through our whole being, circulating our every fibre, just like the vital fluid that circulates the body bringing nutrients to various parts, nourishing tired, dilapidated organs. That life-giving commodity is blood without which life would indeed be non-existent.
It is an undeniable fact we need to see the funny side of things to make life that much more pleasant. You surely must agree that without a dab of funniness now and then, just like seasoning in the right manner, the right amount of wit can and does enrich our lives.

It has the power to heal individuals, whole nations, to make enemies into friends. So widespread is the curative power of humour that Bob Newhart (1929 -), the famous American comedian, believes frankly that 'Laughter gives us distance.

It allows us to step back from an episode in our lives, deal with it and then move on'. How true are those words when applied to a war situation!

Ron Goldstein[10] provides valuable information about a humorous incident. Briefly he served in the forces from

---

[10] Ron Goldstein, WW2 People's War. Courtesy BBC

27

1942-47 reaching the rank of W/Corporal. He was highly decorated. His words are expressed below:

'Paddy was awarded the MM (Military Medal). Briggs (5ft 1in) and Thirkil (6ft 2in) from Yorkshire were our "stars" at many squadron concerts, as we had time for concerts prior to embarking for Italy from North Africa, and always regaled us with humorous songs in the style of Gert and Daisy which went down well with all of the Officers and other ranks. One day the MPs (Military Police) showed up with a complaint that "someone" had been impersonating MPs in the City of Bone and gaining free drinks - and other favours!'

While the quality of humour is as universal and as varied as human nature itself, it can truly be said that, like human beings, who are all 'kinds and creeds', we also have an uncanny ability to express ourselves in all 'shapes and forms'. A serious incident in one country might tickle one person's 'funny bone', will not be seen as hilarious in a different country. Even countries that are considered neighbours will find different things amusing.

At times citizens in a country make jokes about each other and at themselves. Look around you: there is conclusive evidence that 'the more you find out about the world, the more opportunities there are to laugh at it'. Those words by Bill Nye, a compère on an American TV programme, find their expression in many of the stories in this book. He goes on to emphasise, 'Humour is everywhere, in that there's irony in just about anything a human does'.

For example, in this day of political correctness, is there a population who will think it funny to poke fun at themselves? And yet the Irish stand as a beacon of 'taking the mickey' out of their own country and of themselves. Why do they take such pleasure in self humiliation? Well, it is all for the 'crack' (also 'craic'). In fact, Noel Slevin a reporter with the *Donegal on Sunday* shows he is willing to carry on this tradition and will not bow to the PC brigade. What do you think of this joke by him?

'A pilot was flying in a hot air balloon and was lost somewhere over Limerick in Ireland. He looked down and saw a farmer out in a field and shouted down.

"Hello there, where am I?"

The Irish farmer looked up. "Oh, you can't fool me, you're up there in that little basket."'[11]

---

11 Cartoon by Jordon Krawczyk.

29

Does it not bring a smile to your face? Do you not want to burst out laughing? Then, just as you are laughing your head off, Noel fires off an extra round of Irish jokes from his vast reserves by telling a further 'shaggy dog story'. He continues:

'During the first world war a spy was dropped into an Irish village with instructions to meet up with a contact by the name of Flynn. He was told that the recognition code to use was, "It looks like rain".

The first man he met was a farmer - he asked where he could find Mr Flynn.

"Now, Sir", said the farmer, "which Mr Flynn would that be, as we have a number of Flynns in this village? We have Father O'Flynn, Dr Flynn, Judge Flynn, Flynn the undertaker, Flynn the postman, Flynn the chemist, Flynn the mechanic, Flynn the vet... in fact I'm Flynn too. I'm farmer Flynn."

The spy had an idea and said, "It looks like rain."

"Ah", smiled the farmer, "you'll be wanting Flynn the spy".'

Had you been feeling slightly depressed would that joke not lift your spirits? Better than any pill a doctor can give to cheer you up?

If planet earth was full of Irish comedians, would drug companies who sell 'happy pills' be put out of business?

Oh, you may find that hard to believe and say, 'Come on, I know that this is a tongue in cheek joke'. True, this is a genuine Irish laughable tradition and they can make a joke out of any situation.

Have you not honestly found this to be the case? When you put the cat out at night do you not give a wry smile and thank God for the Irish?

Die Laughing – War Humour

Colin Jacobs from Norfolk tells about a factual incident that actually occurred in 1942. It is told with all the wit that shows how paranoid people can be in a war situation:

'In 1942 Lowestoft was being bombed badly and my Grandfather (David Jacobs, who died in 1995) was on leave. A neighbour in May Road in Lowestoft had heard the ticking of an unexploded bomb in her back garden. When the police arrived and joined the bomb disposal engineers they began searching the garden for the bomb. After a while my Granddad looked up onto the washing line and saw that the "ticking" was in fact the washing line beating against the washing pole in the wind.'

What an idiot he must have felt. Can you not sympathise with him? How many times have we all said and done things only to find that we have got the wrong end of the stick?

How foolish we felt then. But that is not all. Colin Jacobs has more 'ways of making us laugh'. He wrote a further true story:

'Fred Cook was a well known naturalist in Lowestoft and one night he was arrested as a spy.

'He was seen by onlookers to shine a torch up onto buildings and was followed stalking the church yard, looking to collect secret documents buried there by other spies.

'On arrival of the Lowestoft constabulary he was questioned as to his motives. He produced his jars of moths and his torch and pronounced that he was looking for nocturnal insects. He was sent home but his torch was confiscated for the duration of the war.'

31

George Korankye

Enough of the hilarity from Colin Jacobs. Let's now look at things from a Scottish perspective. Onward to Aberdeen, which is home to 'tight fisted Aberdonians'. What about the Scottish accent - does it not cause many a headache, not just for English residents but especially those living overseas? Jean Gordon from Perth goes on to share a true story. She says:

'My Father served in the trenches and, although he never talked of the war, he had a droll sense of humour and told his family a few stories to give us a laugh. The one I remember best concerned the troops shopping in a local bakery.

'As you may know, the French word "trois" meaning three is pronounced exactly the same as the Scots word "twa" meaning two. So the joke was that 'they Frenchies canna coont (cannot count) - you ask for twa rolls and they gie ye (give you) three.'

For the benefit of those reading this book who do not understand 'broad Scots', the actual last sentence should be read as 'Those French people cannot count, you ask for two rolls and they give you three'.

What generous folk those 'Frenchies' are. Maybe they did understand and were only trying to be hospitable to a total stranger. Funny, it's not only the Frenchies who 'canny coont' - there are English people who 'canny' understand the Scots. It seems funny, therefore, that in May 2008 the UK Government announced that skilled migrants who want to be employed in Britain will have to be able to be competent in English. The Immigration Minister Liam Byrne said the main thrust of this directive was to enable British workers to get a better chance of obtaining employment.

Speaking English? There are 'natives' of the UK who cannot string two words together, who just mumble like newborn babies. These NEDS (Non Educated Delinquents)[12] could do with a short sharp English lesson too, Mr Byrne, so please take note. To prove that not everyone can speak the Queen's English, consider this letter by Ken Buchanan:[13]

'The Influx of Polish nationals reminded me of a conversation I heard during the early years of the war. A group of Glasgow lassies were chatting up Polish troops through the railings of Bellahouston Park, where the Poles were stationed prior to joining our armed forces. "If youse yins teach us yins Polish, we'll teach youse yins English". Nuff said.'

For the benefit of non-Glaswegians, the translation is 'If you lot teach us Polish, we will teach you lot English'. Easy if you happen to be from Glasgow, not so easy if you happen to be from Poland. They may as well be speaking Klingon[14] or Swahili. It would not take a rocket scientist to deduce that the poor Poles did not have a clue what those 'lassies' meant. Would you agree with that statement?

It immediately hits you like a brick hurled in anger that what is understood as 'English' in Glasgow is not actually English and, as if that was not enough, only in

---

12 Rosie Kane (2003-2007) an ex MP of the Scottish Parliament denounced the use of NED in Scotland to describe hooligans. In her view this was offensive. NEDS made the Burberry an iconic item for 'hoodlums'. They were usually involved in self destructive and anti-social behaviour.

13 Courtesy *Sunday Post*: 25 May 2008, letters page.

14 Klingon was a language spoken by aliens in the Star Trek series.

Glasgow do words have different meanings. By way of an example, you don't go to the shops or supermarket for food or groceries. No, you go for 'messages'. To the ordinary man in the street the word message has nothing to do with food, but not so in Glasgow. In English, a message means something entirely different.

A different word to illustrate this further is 'wee'. This is not a rude name for a normal bodily function, it simply means small. Look at the name of the person who sent the letter. His name is Ken. Well, in Scotland 'Ken' is not always the name of a person; it can mean directions, as in 'Do you ken where to go to get a decent kebab?' It could indicate the person understands what you are saying: 'I ken that was what you were trying to say'. Or conversely: 'I dinny ken', meaning 'I don't understand'. What chance did those poor 'wee' Polish soldiers have in being understood outside Glasgow if they were taught 'Glaswegian English'?

Going back in Scottish history, did you know that there was animosity between Clans? The Clan system engendered loyalty similar to what the tribal systems of Africa do today. Miles Noonan[15] shares a tale of the rivalry between the MacDonalds and the Campbells. Any Scottish school child worth his 'low salt' is well aware of the historic slaughter that has become known as the Massacre of Glencoe. To understand the joke that follows, it is necessary to brief you of the background to this slaughter and which led to the animosity between the MacDonalds and the Campbells.

Scotland was at one time a nation divided by clan structure and by regions, the Highlands and Lowlands. By the latter part of the 17th century, this division

---

15 *Tales from the Mess* by Miles Noonan (1983) p67.

resulted in one side supporting the Royalists and King William III of England or, as he was more popularly known, William of Orange abbreviated colloquially to 'King Billy'. The others supported the Jacobite cause, which has been romanticised in novels and history with its figure of Bonnie Prince Charlie.

The exploits of Charles Edward Stuart the Young Pretender - as he became known - to the throne was immortalised in song. After his defeat at the Battle of Culloden (1746), which effectively put a stop to any future Stuart usurping the throne, he fled to the Isle of Skye in Scotland and then subsequently found exile in France. The *Skye Boat Song* is a romanticised tribute to his lost cause.

Skye Boat Song

(Chorus)
Speed, bonnie boat, like a bird on the wing,
Onward! the sailors cry;
Carry the lad that's born to be King
Over the sea to Skye.

Loud the winds howl, loud the waves roar,
Thunderclaps rend the air;
Baffled, our foes stand by the shore,
Follow they will not dare.
Speed, bonnie boat, like a bird on the wing,
Onward! the sailors cry;
Carry the lad that's born to be King
Over the sea to Skye.

(Chorus)

George Korankye

Though the waves leap, soft shall ye sleep,
Ocean's a royal bed.
Rocked in the deep, Flora will keep
Watch by your weary head.
Speed, bonnie boat, like a bird on the wing,
Onward! the sailors cry;
Carry the lad that's born to be King
Over the sea to Skye.

(Chorus)

Many's the lad fought on that day,
Well the Claymore could wield,
When the night came, silently lay
Dead in Culloden's field.
Speed, bonnie boat, like a bird on the wing,
Onward! the sailors cry;
Carry the lad that's born to be King
Over the sea to Skye.

(Chorus)

Burned are their homes, exile and death
Scatter the loyal men;
Yet ere the sword cool in the sheath
Charlie will come again.
Speed, bonnie boat, like a bird on the wing,
Onward! the sailors cry;
Carry the lad that's born to be King
Over the sea to Skye.

(Chorus)

Sir Harold Boulton (1859 – 1935)

The Jacobite rebellions stirred up feelings of Scottish independence, the remnants of which have survived down to our current times. The British National Anthem at one time bore testimony to this fact. Although not universally known, there were at least six verses to this anthem. At national occasions only one is sung. However, the sixth verse goes as follows:

Lord grant that Marshall Wade,
May by thy might aid,
Victory bring.
May he sedition hush,
And like a torrent rush,
Rebellious Scots to crush,
God save the Queen!

The reference to Wade was regarding his role as one of the British commanders during the Jacobite rebellions (1715 and 1745), which became known as the 'Fifteen' and 'Forty five' uprisings.

The beginnings of the massacre started when 120 men, led by Captain Campbell of Glenlyon, travelled to Glencoe. He stated that his sole intention was the collection of back taxes. In this inhospitable terrain, the McDonalds gave them shelter. To verify that their intentions were honourable, they actually produced authentic military documents. This act was accepted without question, partly because Glenlyon's niece was related to Alexander MacDonald by marriage.

However, on the famous day of 12 February the order was given to murder the MacDonalds. This was carried out the next morning and, although it was intended to get rid of all the clan, some managed to escape. The Campbell guests who had accepted the hospitality of the

MacDonalds killed thirty-eight from the Clan MacDonald of Glencoe, the rationale given was that they had not shown allegiance to 'King Billy'. It is reputed that a further forty women and children died of exposure after their homes were burned. Thus, the animosity between these two Clans was still ongoing during WW2. The hereditary chief of the murdered Campbells is the Duke of Argyll.

With the background of the story of the slaughter in mind, the wisecrack comments attached to Noonan's story can be now be fully appreciated.

The story unfolds in 1940 when a special training school had been established at Inveraray to train potential saboteurs. This part of Scotland is particularly suited for this kind of vocation. It has rough mountain terrain which helped the soldiers to develop stamina by increasing their lung capacity; secluded wooded areas to assist them to perfect camouflaging techniques and deep lochs which enabled potential recruits to be skilful and 'swim like fishes'. In fact, there is no area in Scotland more suited to this kind of endurance training and polishing of survival skills.

It is one thing having the right territory to practice your skills and quite another to have experienced staff to instruct potential recruits. To the rescue came the Royal Argyll and Sutherland Highlanders, who had arrived with the Royal Marines. Now, think of the area where the training was occurring, consider too the name of the regiment 'The Highlanders'. Where do you think most of their recruits came from? Yes, from the local area. These people knew the land like the back of their hands. They had grown up in it, stalked deer perhaps for the landowner in whose estates they lived. Some of them may very well have been poachers, helping themselves surreptitiously to game they felt was rightly theirs by virtue of being born on the land.

It is also likely others probably just enjoyed the land of their birth, taking full advantage of its breathtaking beauty by virtue of snow-covered mountains reminiscent of an old greying man, landscaped floral covered fields, bubbling fresh water brooks that twisted among the land feeding the fertile lochs with its 'salmon offspring'. The remainder may have engaged in mountain walking, climbing the various Munros.[16] There may very well have been farmers and shepherds among this band.

The binding force for this unit was not so much their professions or station in life but where they came from. This fact enabled them to pass on much-needed, well-honed skills to their fellows, the Marines.

In most training colleges or universities, it is customary, once the year's intake of new recruits have gained their 'wings', to have a passing out parade. In some occupations this is called 'graduation day' whereby successful students proudly display their hard won degrees, or in the case of the army their berets, to show to all and sundry that they have successfully persevered in their assignments. A wonderful day indeed for all those passing out and for any invited quests, usually family and friends.

Have you ever been to a passing out parade, a graduation, school prize-giving day or a school sports

---

16 To qualify as a Munro in Scotland a mountain must be over 3,000 feet (914.4 metres). Their name is taken from the person credited with their compilation, Sir Hugh T Munro (1856–1919), who collated and catalogued 'Munro' tables. Currently there are 284 'Munros'. The most well-known one is Ben Nevis and the one hardest to find is Sgurr Dearg on the Island of Skye, where Bonnie Prince Charlie fled to after 'The '45' rebellion.

day? Perhaps you have been a proud parent who, with a grin as wide as a Cheshire cat, gave your daughter away at her wedding? We all have special days which we have attended that made us puff out our chests with pride. Is that not the case? We can then put ourselves in the shoes of those recruits and imagine their feelings. They had been through thick and thin, endured circumstances they thought they could never survive; they could now breathe a sigh of relief. Wow! They had made it, finally passed!

Anyway, as the end of the ceremonies approached and after all the speeches, some of which invariably will be boring, the hereditary chief of the Campbells stood up to do his usual speech. Have you ever seen the Oscars? What happens when an actor or an actress is awarded a prize? There are the obligatory speeches, some good, others bad, and then there are endless downright diatribes which can be either boring or a tad unbelievable. Human nature being what it is, the Duke would have followed the same procedure. Anyway, at the end of the discourse the Duke of Argyll removed his cap and, as is customary in the armed forces, he called for three cheers.

Noonan reports: 'In the brief pause before the first "Hip, hip", a stern, deviant voice came from the ranks of the Argyles:

"MacDonalds stand fast," ordered a senior NCO (Non Commissioned Officer) bleakly. They did.'

It appeared that the MacDonalds had the memory of an elephant, for they would not bow to the Duke who, they felt, was a representative of the treacherous Campbells. Is this tongue in cheek wit or an unforgiving nature? It depends on how it is interpreted. It could very well have been just community banter, a kind of good old friendly rivalry, the type which exists between various football clubs in the UK.

Die Laughing – War Humour

An example is that between Chelsea and Tottenham, or the two Uniteds in Manchester, or the 'Toon Army' of Newcastle United FC and the 'Mackems' of Sunderland AFC, or Glasgow Celtic and Rangers. Certainly, although a minority at times do go beyond the pale and use this friendly banter as a front for inexcusable violence, the majority see this as they are, just friendly on the field rivalry quickly forgotten once the game is finished. Fans will then go their respective ways in a pleasant manner.

In fact, it is not unknown for rival team supporters to work together, play together and at times to be married to each other. No fisticuffs carried on there. If the story is perceived in this light then it is indeed funny.

The expertise of the Highlanders is not far-fetched. Indeed, David Turnbull recounts:

'There was an exercise where there was a team of saboteurs which was a platoon in strength (we'd call them insurgents nowadays). Up against this platoon (of 20 men) was a company of home guards (about 120 men) who were supposed to whittle out the insurgents who were hiding and eliminate them. But it all went wrong. On the day of the exercise only four of the platoon could turn up as it was harvest time. They decided to continue with the exercise. It was four against 120 and they didn't have a chance. However, they were all poachers and had hiding places and holes dug all over the place.

'The idea was that officers would watch as the home guards and saboteurs shouted "bang, bang!" with empty rifles as they pretended to shoot each other. The officers would decide who was dead. The action started with the four saboteurs doing well, killing many of the company and then running for cover. The action became more amazing as the four saboteurs whittled the company

41

down to zero men left alive. They wiped them out without losing a man. Four beat 120 mercilessly.

'Much was learnt about saboteurs and insurgents, which is probably still used nowadays. They all had a few pints of beer together and had a good laugh about the whole exercise.'

Leaving Scotland and travelling south to England, what do we discover? We encounter a breed the Scots call the 'Sassenachs' (English). Have they not from time immemorial poked fun at their northern neighbours, the Scots? What well-known 'pet name' do they call them? Is it not 'Jocks'? And how are 'Jocks' usually portrayed? By and large as inarticulate, incoherent drunks. Focus your eye on the cartoon's date.

Text: '**Eh, but I had a rare time last year – R A was at ma cousin MacWhuskie's a whole fortnight, an' a didna once ken a was theer!**' *Punch*, 21 January 1914.[17]

---

[17] Reproduced with permission of Punch ltd; www.punch.co.uk

'Canny' or 'cautious' is an additional term used to describe Scots. Some will go as far as to say that this can mean being overcautious.

A well-known joke circulating the pubs is: 'How was copper wire invented? Two Scotsmen were fighting over a penny'. Funny, no mention of Aberdonians there, eh?

So when Gordon Brown, the 'Canny Scot', was in charge of Britain's purse strings as Chancellor of the Exchequer (1997-2007) many thought that no one was better qualified to look after Britain's economy. Were they correct? History answers that question vividly.

It is also well known that French and Germans not only see things differently, but also do not spot the same punch lines. The British also label the Germans as 'dour' and always getting up early while on holiday to put their towels on the best seats nearest the beach or swimming pool. Differences in humour definitely exist among differing countries. Collating information for this book proved this point. Consider the following:

The author contacted the German War Graves Commission (Volksbund Deutsche Kriegsgräberfürsorge in German) for statistics and stories for this publication. They readily supplied the former. However, in response to humorous incidents, Karin Bassti said of her organisation '…we must admit that we had to think twice about your unusual wish to connect war and humour'. However, this is not indicative of the whole nation as there were and still are German cartoonists and comics, both male and female.

Consider Helen Cleary[18] who passes on '…a genuine newspaper cutting of the time from the *Bournemouth Evening Echo*. Whether this German was a fanatic is not

---

18 Helen Cleary, WW2 People's War. Courtesy BBC.

known - I like to think he had a wicked sense of humour!'

Helen goes on to expand why she felt this way about the German POW. The story was relayed by Irene Graham of Boscombe who had the company of a German POW assigned to take care of her garden.

This POW, a model prisoner, meticulously tended her garden, week in week out. However, when the war ended and he was repatriated to Germany, something quite strange occurred in her garden.

Irene graham[19] says: 'He was repatriated at the end of 1945. He'd always seemed a nice friendly chap, but when the crocuses came up in the middle of our lawn in February 1946, they spelt out, "Heil Hitler".'

Contrast the terse German War Graves Commission reaction above for stories to the British response.

The Western Front Association's answer to the identical correspondence to their President which was then referred to Ronald Clifton their Historical Information Officer solicited this magnanimous reply:

'There are various books compiled from soldiers' reminiscences, such as Lyn Macdonald's book *1915: The Death of Innocence* which has a story about attempts to disguise a medical officer's white horse with various improvised dyes.

'Jonathan Nicholls' book *Cheerful Sacrifice* about the Battle of Arras in 1917 also has some interesting reminiscences, including those of Cpl Alf Razzell, Royal Fusiliers, on page 111 and 204-208.

'*Sniping in France* by Major H Hesketh-Prichard also includes some lighter touches, Chapter 9, involving several sightings of a cat in the German front line.

---

19 Irene Graham, WW2 People's War. Courtesy BBC.

'There are two older books by Miles Noonan, *Tales from the Mess*, which contain stories from the 1880s to the 1980s, and *Salute the Soldier* by Captain Eric Bush may also be useful to you.

'Richard Holmes' recent books *Tommy* and *Dusty Warriors* also include lighter touches from soldiers.

'Even the British *Official History: Military Operations, France and Flanders* by Maj-Gen Sir James Edmonds is not without its lighter moments. In the 1918 Volume III there is a footnote on page 197 referring to the action at La Becque on 20 June: 'Telephone communication was at once laid down from the front line. One young officer sent a message, "Have captured all objectives but a bottle of whiskey would help us to hold on". He got it.'

'Another story in the same volume relates to the capture of Meteren on 19 July (page 212). It describes how the divisional commander used a bicycle to go to the front line to see how matters were progressing, but when he was ready to return to HQ he found that his bicycle has disappeared.'

Would you agree with the above assumption that differences in humour pertaining to different countries do exist? It can unequivocally be stated in line with anecdotal evidence obtained over the years that, in general, Germans do not possess the same humour as the British, Scottish, Irish, French or the Welsh.

So universal is humour that it has been said by the French novelist who wrote under the alias of Colette (1873-1954): 'Total absence of humour renders life impossible'.

The Irish, at times incorrectly described as being 'as thick as two short planks', will show by their own jokes that maybe, yes, just perhaps, they are not as 'thick' as

45

some make them out to be. A 'thick Paddy' attitude can at times be plain stupid, as Noel Slevin shows in this story with a twist:

'The English Captain of a Royal Navy ship received a radio call from Paddy.

"Please alter your course 43 degrees to the West to avoid a collision."

The Captain replied, "Suggest you change your course to 43 degrees East to avoid a collision."

"Ah now, I can't be doing that," said Paddy calmly. "So please alter your course 43 degrees to the West to avoid a collision."

"I am the Captain of a Royal Navy aircraft carrier and I say alter your course."

"And I say again," replied Paddy, "You should steer her over a bit."

The Captain was furious. "Good God, man, I am the Captain of Britain's biggest aircraft carrier with enough firepower to blast you out of the water. Who on earth are you?"

"I'm Paddy."

"Paddy who?" shouted the Captain.

"Paddy the lighthouse keeper. Please alter your course".'

Stupidity is not the preserve of the Irish. David Turnbull from Northumberland recollects:

'There was a home guard exercise somewhere on a beach in Northumberland. It was hand grenade practice and this is a true story. One of the blokes practicing was a farm labourer and not that bright. He was told to take out the pin and throw it, which he did. Unfortunately he

46

threw away the pin instead of the grenade and it blew two fingers off his hand.'

Successful comedians in one country can find it extremely difficult to woo an audience in a new land, a fact impossible to deny. Irrespective of which country examined, we find a common denominator. Do you know, in every country you look at you will always find someone who can cheer a worried soul by their wit? They will apply the solution to a problem, according to journalist Edgar Howe (1853-1937), who said: 'If you don't learn to laugh at trouble, you won't have anything to laugh at when you're old'.

That fact is echoed by Elsa Maxwell (1883-1963), an American gossip columnist, who goes on to reiterate: 'Laugh at yourself first, before anyone can'. If the people featured herein had not applied that adage all those decades ago, we today would not be enjoying an unlikely fruitage of their adversity, thus proving true Mark Twain's (1835-1910) words: 'The human race has one really effective weapon, and that is laughter'.

Yes, there is no doubting it, 'he (or she) who laughs, lasts!' so says author and poet John Masefield (1878-1967), a theory proved true by those who came through the greatest adversity humans have ever faced - the Great War of 1914.

Scrutinise any state in the world, scan their newspapers and what will you come across? Talented illustrators and cartoonists who apply the old adage: 'A picture paints a thousand words' and who, with the stroke of a pen, can get heads nodding in agreement. Or how about the writers, with their sarcastic and biting wit, who can bring a wry smile to a reader silently flicking from end to end a newspaper, magazine, or hardback in a public place? How many times have you, either on a train or a bus, heard someone chuckling over what they are reading? Then there is the complete stranger who uninvited, yes unprompted, wants to share one of their jokes with you.

What do you think of this, from Geoff Horton an RAF personnel based at St Athan? No, it is not a true story, but it gives you a flavour of what is to come. It draws on his RAF background:

'A teacher gave her class of 11-year-olds an assignment: to get their parents to tell them a story with a moral at the end of it. The next day the kids came back and one by one began to tell their stories.

Ashley said, "My father's a farmer and we have a lot of egg laying hens. One time we were taking our eggs to market in a basket on the front seat of the car when we hit a big bump in the road and all the eggs got broken."

"What's the moral of that story?" asked the teacher.

"Don't put all your eggs in one basket!"

"Very good," said the teacher.

Next, little Sarah raised her hand and said, "Our family are farmers too. But we raise chickens for the meat market. One day we had a dozen eggs, but when they hatched we only got ten live chicks, and the moral to this story is, don't count your chickens before they're hatched."

"That was a fine story, Sarah. Little Johnny, do you have a story to share?"

"Yes. My daddy told me this story about my Aunty Sharon who was a RAF flight engineer on a plane in the Gulf War and her plane got hit. She had to bail out over enemy territory and all she had was a bottle of whisky, a machine gun and a machete. She drank the whisky on the way down so it wouldn't break and then she landed right in the middle of 100 Iraqi soldiers. She killed seventy of them with the machine gun until she ran out of ammunition. Then she killed twenty more with the machete until the blade broke. And then she killed the last ten with her bare hands."

"Good heavens, that's some story," said the horrified teacher. "What kind of moral did your daddy tell you from that horrible story?"

"STAY WELL AWAY FROM AUNTY SHARON WHEN SHE HAS BEEN DRINKING."'

The Iraq War, also known as Gulf War 2 (2003-present), shows the skills that the ordinary man on the street has. Open any newspaper, read any magazine and you will not find the poem below in them. It will not be critiqued by any expert with initials as long as this sentence and yet does it not show a brilliance that is down to earth? Judge for yourself.

This poem, called *Hussanga*, was penned by David Hawkins in 2008.

Hussanga

George Bush and Tony Blair decided
To pay a visit to Iraq,
Then they could tell the people,
The reason for the attack.

The Iraqis came in their thousands,
To see them land on Iraqi soil.
They all shouted, 'Hussanga, Hussanga,'
When Bush said, 'It's nothing to do with oil.'

George Korankye

Tony Blair thought the Iraqi people
Were in a very friendly mood,
For they all shouted, 'Hussanga, Hussanga,'
When he promised them all free food.

Bush said 'Your land will prosper,
Now that Saddam's regime is gone.'
Again they shouted, 'Hussanga, Hussanga,'
When he said, 'There will be work for everyone.'

Both Bush and Blair were delighted
There were handshakes all around,
Then an interpreter said to George Bush,
'Don't step in that Hussanga on the ground.'

How true were Mark Twain's words: 'Thousands of geniuses live and die undiscovered - either by themselves or by others'. These words find their application in a young talent the author discovered while compiling this volume. In fact look at page [29], which is about this young novice who, without any formal training, was given the commission by the author to 'cartoonise' some of the stories featured. As you peruse this publication, look for his work. It is initialled JK, which is short for Jordon Krawczyk.

To be fair, we've mentioned the 'Jocks' (oops sorry, the Scots), the 'Sassenach' (oh drat! the English) and the 'Paddies' (excuse me, I meant the Irish). There seems to be a nationality missing - oh, it must be the Welsh!

There are many euphemisms associated with the Welsh but, as this is a family book, we will stick to the ones that refer to their names. Who can honestly pronounce a Welsh place name without getting tongue-tied? What is the longest place name in Britain?

Llanfairpwllgwyngyllgogerychwyrndrobwllllantysilio gogogoch, which contains 58 letters. Yes, 58 letters. Now try saying that without taking in a breath! No wonder they are such good singers - with such place names you need good lungs. Perhaps their secret weapon has been their language. This place is located where? In Anglesey, an island which lays claim to being Welsh.

George Glover, a young 17-year-old employed as a firer at Plodders sheds in Bolton during WW2, remembers a funny incident. He writes:

'There were a number of Welsh men at Plodders Croft, many with identical names, for example Owen Thomas or Thomas Owen…even Thomas Thomas…but there were also a large number of men who went by the name of Dick Hughes, so that in order to know who your mate was, they were all nicknamed from where they had originated from, e.g., Abergele Dick, Penman Dick (Penmanwaer) and even Dogger Dick (a well-known peeping tom) of which a well-known tale of him was known by all at the yard…

'Dogger Dick was relieved at Crewe and was waiting, on a dark, shadowed evening platform, for a train back to Manchester, when he spotted a 'couple' leaning against a wall in the shadows. He told his mate to keep quiet and he proceeded to WATCH the said couple for about 20 minutes before the Manchester train ran in and was *HUMILIATED* in front of his fireman when Dogger saw the COUPLE being loaded into the guards van…for THE COUPLE were actually *TWO SMALL 6 ft ROLLS OF LINO* waiting to be loaded onto the Manchester train for destinations in the Manchester area, etc…

'*OH WHAT A LET DOWN* and humiliation for *DOGGER* when the tale was revealed later at Plodders Croft depot…poor *DOGGER*'.

George Korankye

The giving of special names appears to be correct. In fact, Miles Noonan in his *Tales from the mess* reports of a soldier given the suffix '67' after his name. It appears there were so many Welsh soldiers in his regiment called Williams that the only way to ensure mix-ups were kept to a minimum was to give each William a number following his name.[20]

The soldier being discussed was 'Williams 67'. It would appear George Glover[21] was carrying on a tradition of inventing some kind of formula to help them remember Welsh names. What kind of nation gives its inhabitants names that are so alike that a formula or a mnemonic has to be used as a memory aid? Can you imagine being in India where nearly every surname is a Singh? What challenges there would be in remembering names there, eh?

Then there is the north of Scotland where the name McLeod is as common as muck. Imagine being a schoolteacher with twenty McLeod's in class. Just as well the North is sparsely populated.

The government during the war years went back to basics. It recognised that humour can be very effective in binding the nation. In fact, *Readers Digest* has a special section entitled 'Laughter the best medicine' which deals with situations that it feels will warm the 'cockles of the

---

20 Although there are 58 letters in this name, in reality there are only 51; e.g., ll, ng and ch can be combined. There is some debate as to why the Welsh came up with this place name. Some say it was because they wanted to be credited with the longest place name in the UK. Difficulty in pronunciation resulted in it being called Llanfair-pwllgwyngyll. Even this caused problems so it was called Llanfairpwll. Colloquially it is Llanfair PG.

21 George, now a 'mature man', typed, using a 'strike' typewriter, pages of stories. He also drew countless images. Sadly due to space not all could be included. 'George, look out for the next volume!'

heart'. This title may well have been derived from a religious compilation which states 'A cheerful heart is good medicine, but a crushed spirit dries up the bones' Proverbs 17: 22, The Holy Bible, New International Version. A very interesting exposition.

Scientific data acquired over the years proves that laughter can indeed 'do exactly as it says on the tin' and make you feel better about a situation. We know that you can get a qualification for practically anything under the sun in the 21st century, but it is not just 'quacks' who found the healing power of humour beneficial. No, it is not just 'quackery' medicine; it is indeed taken seriously because there are actually hospitals (one is in Australia) that have clown doctors.

What can humour actually do? It can help a person's psychological, emotional and mental state. It has the potential to actually help in the healing process. Science has discovered that it actually has the ability to help the old ticker not just beat faster but perhaps pound longer.

When you laugh a chain reaction is started in your body. We know 'the leg bone is connected to the thigh bone and the thigh bone is…' You can probably finish the rhyme. What this rhyme is saying is that the human body is interdependent, which means it works together so that one part of the body affects the other parts.

There is thus a cumulative or a snowballing effect: the longer this situation goes on the more the person will either gain or lose. So if a person is happy it has been found that this boosts their immune system; that person will produce what have been called 'T cells'. These cells have also been shown to lower cortisol levels, which can be harmful if you have too much of this. Why? Because cortisol is what is called a stress hormone - it makes you get up uptight and if you are uptight what happens? Well your blood boils, you get all hot under the collar and steam starts coming out of your ears. If this goes on for too long, the body's immune system is weakened.

It stands to reason, therefore, that anything that can help you keep your cool must be good for you. When that happens then your immune system is built up. A good old hearty laugh does all this because it produces killer cells. These killer cells are well named because they can kill rogue cells that attack the body.

You can immediately see for yourself how a good laugh helps to relieve stress, alleviate pain and relax the muscles. How? Basically, your muscles are only capable of two movements. They are either relaxed or tense or, as doctors say, they either contract or relax. So if you are at ease then your muscles are relaxed. This means you are less likely to be depressed.

A side effect of a good laugh is therefore that people have a positive outlook on life, and is this not better than any pill? Is this view accurate, backed up by science with consistent studies confirming this approach?

An old Italian saying goes: 'He who has the courage to laugh is almost as much a master of the world as he who is ready to die'. The same thoughts reverberate in the Tuscarora Indians of America, who say: 'They are not dead who live in the hearts of those they leave behind'.

A departed person who is remembered with warmth, their dislikes and likes recollected with cheerful sentimental emotions, will bring back happy memories for those who have this attitude making it easier to evoke ic laughter. We have in fact conjured up colours to eople's feelings and attitudes. For example, we of feeling blue, in the dark, in the pink, ale or white, or having a bright outlook, as button'. Conversely, we may describe ourselves as having 'black moods' when we are depressed.

In Scotland there is a saying that goes 'black affronted', meaning thoroughly ashamed. All these colours emphasise feelings and emotions. No wonder the Chinese say 'A smile will gain you ten more years', a notion not at odds with the Mexicans who state 'He who lives with hope dies happy'.

Another offshoot of war is that it can produce amazing coincidences. Consider what happened to Mrs Stuart, who became a VAD nurse in 1939. She elucidates as follows:

'In 1945 I arrived in Calcutta. I booked into a hotel and was given a huge room with three beds and the most enormous spider I have ever seen on the wall above the remaining one! No mosquito net was provided so I pulled the bedclothes over my head and hoped for the best. In the morning I discovered to my amazement that, in one of the other beds, was my sister-in-law, whom I had never met. I still phone her every Sunday!'

But why will the government try and make people cheerful in a war situation? Well, if you are laughing with someone are you all not at one? Are you not drawn closer together? So laughing together draws people together. It's a case of 'all for one and one for all', as the musketeers said. However, there is a difference between laughing together and laughing about others. This kind of laughter can create animosity which, if it is not curtailed, can lead to prejudices and hurt feelings.

For example, to denigrate a nation can create bad feelings. In time, that type of laughter can lead to prejudice and stereotyping.

An example of this fact is a story by John Wood Cowling from Corby. He relates:

'When I was a kid in the 1940s, this old guy lost his leg below the knee in 1916 in World War One. The old guy was a peg-leg, he was single and lived alone. He had a wee pension and never worked again. In the pub a guy said to him, "Get up to the hospital, they will give you a new metal leg and you can wear a pair of shoes." He went and got his free leg. Luckily he had a pal who had lost the other leg from him and had the same size feet. From then on they went to the Market and bought a pair of shoes between them!

'The same guy kept his peg-leg for emergencies; he would run out of money two days before his pension day so he would pawn his leg, putting on his peg-leg as he liked his beer.

'We cruel kids would chase after him, saying "pawn yer leg, pawn yer leg!"'

Notice in hindsight how John Cowling now views his actions as cruel and regrets his words. However, at that time he thought the whole incident funny.

Perhaps it was because he was only a kid, and the attitudes prevailing at the time may have all played a part in his tomfoolery.

Let's be honest, how many prejudices did we have or cherish in the past which we now no longer hold onto? Conversely, how many have we acquired because of outside influences, be they from the media, family or friends, which affect our way of thinking?

Laughter has a unique ability to divert people from what they are doing. By this I mean if you are experiencing pain and someone tells you a good joke which makes you laugh, you will not focus on the pain so much.

A story which proves this point is that of Sergeant Ike Franklin, who relives his experiences in the Army in Italy from 1943. He recollects the constant shelling and the inability to sleep. His mate, who was with him at the time, was getting exasperated through the constant shelling and he turned to Ike and said:

'Ike, what are we going to do?' and I said, "We're going to stay right here". And he said, "What about the shells?" And I said, "Well, they're going to kill me whether I'm asleep or awake. I'm going to have some sleep". And that was the only damn sleep I got from the time we landed until after I got captured.'[22]

Notice the difference between the soldier accepting with humour his predicament and the other who was frightened. Both were in the same situation and had experienced lack of sleep, an important function of the body if it is to recuperate, especially from stress. Once the situation was accepted, albeit with a tinge of sarcasm, the body was able to relax and sleep like a baby in a battlefield. Unbelievable!

Norman Cousins (1912-1990), who has been known as the father of laughter and a healer, states: 'Hearty laughter is a good way to jog internally without having to go outside'.[23]

However, Cousins was not the first to confirm the benefits of laughter. Lord Byron (1788-1824) said:

---

[22] *Lest We Forget: Forgotten Voices 1914-1945* by Max Arthur (2007) p200. Courtesy Random House Publishing.

[23] www.humourfoundation.com.au.

'Always laugh when you can. It is cheap medicine'. Going further back in history, Lucius Seneca (4BC-65AD), the Roman humorist, said: 'A great step toward independence is a good humoured stomach'.

Wherever you look, be it in religious writings, or work by philosophers, poets, writers, actors or actresses, they all wax lyrically about the benefits of laughter, and who can argue against this.

If we couldn't laugh we would definitely go insane. What are the rewards of laughter? The Koran says: 'He deserves paradise who makes his companions laugh'.

With all these benefits no wonder the government tried to get the nation to see the funny side of things. It realised that 'when you are smiling, the whole world smiles with you' or, as it has been shown by clinical evidence, 'laughter is the best medicine'.

Looking at it from the perspective of dramatist and writer Victor Hugo (1802-1885), 'Laughter is the sun that drives winter from the human face'.

The UK faced an unparalleled 'winter' during times of war, especially the Great War. It badly needed a catalyst that would help the nation see the funny side of things.[24]

Although this book is primarily about humour in the UK, it is beyond its scope to look at humour from all the warring nations during times of war.

The points made, the poems written, the interviews conducted and the stories that have been told could all be the same, were the author to look at humour from the point of view of Germans, Austrians, Russians, Italians - in fact, from all the warring nations.

---

24 For more on the scientific proofs for this view, please see the bibliography pages. For a balanced view of humour from other nations during the war years the reader can look at *World War 2 in Cartoons* by Mark Bryant (1989).

A fitting conclusion to this chapter is a poem by William Maylam.[25]

One kind word can work great wonders.
One small rift can break a cloud.
One brave heart can strengthen many.
And one smile can cheer a crowd.

Why did a whole nation need cheering? The following chapter will provide some insight.

---

[25] The author was given access to William Maylam's war diaries by his son Peter. These contained over 100 pages of poems, jokes and personal thoughts. They were scanned 'warts and all' and portions are shown throughout this book. William, according to Peter, served in North Africa (1941-1945).

Chapter 2

Uniqueness

'Great fires erupt from tiny sparks'
Libyan proverb

In the field of human existence there have been situations that call for the 'true metal' of a person, group or even nations to be shown. The 20th century, called for an endurance and strength of character never before experienced in the field of human history. That scenario was World War I, which a number of historians claim was responsible for the so-called 'bulldog spirit' in the United Kingdom.

The strength of character the nation was forced to discover made its inhabitants glimpse the funnier side of the horrendous circumstances they wholeheartedly embraced. [26] Casualties include those captured, injured or killed.

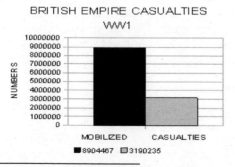

BRITISH EMPIRE CASUALTIES WW1

[26] www.anzacday.org.au & www.spartacus.schoolnet.co.uk/

George Korankye

There is no doubt about it: the copious amount of bloodshed affected everybody.

As far as the majority were concerned, this was going to be a short war; in fact, some said that it would only last six months. It was going to be 'a war to end all wars'. The euphoria that gripped the nation could be likened to a journey to an unknown place, to 'A land that time forgot'.[27]

What people did not realise at the time was that this journey would be similar to a train ride in a picturesque and, at times, unfamiliar and dangerous land littered with camouflaged booby traps, stopping at various stations and picking up passengers on its long journey.

Travellers ranged from businessmen and politicians to the ordinary man in the street. As the length of the journey increased, its commuter list became more varied, embracing reluctant travellers who at times had to be shoved on, just as the guards do on the Japanese bullet train. Others keenly jumped on without any prompting, some going as far as lying to get on this once in a lifetime journey.

The passenger list would go on to include not only a 'who's who' but women, men, children of all ages and even foreigners. All became 'packed to the gunnels'. Then, to lighten its load, as the strain became unbearably heavy, it would unburden itself of unnecessary cargo of humans at times in coffins along its journey.

---

[27] *The Land That Time Forgot* (1975) is a science fiction film of a book of the same name by Edgar Rice Burroughs, published in 1918. The story revolves around The Great War Years (1914-18). A British ship is torpedoed and sinks, and the crew and passengers are taken captive on board a German U-boat. They then travel to a land that time has forgotten. In this mythical land dinosaurs are still roaming the earth.

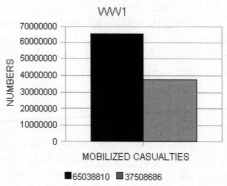

TOTAL COMBATANTS
WW1

Even those who were considered sacrosanct, such as priests and members of religious orders, were considered fair game for 'mickey taking'. By the time WW2 started, making fun of religious figures was acceptable.

From his portfolio gathered from various airmen over the years, Geoff Horton, an RAF personnel based at St Athan, sent this cartoon.

Text: **'I awoke with it this morning, Doc.'**

The First World War was also called the Great War. Why? It was 'Great' due to the colossal number of casualties. Oh! We had had shootouts before then, for example the two Boer Wars (1880-1902), the Napoleonic Wars (1803-1815), the American War of Independence (1775-1783) and, going even further back in history, the Thirty Years' War (1618-1648). The results of such exchanges of hostilities? Sufferings for many, yes! Bringing with it misery for the masses, definitely! Affecting thousands upon thousands of the population, without question!

So in what sense was the First World War a 'Great' War? How different was it from the previous acts of aggression?

It was 'Great' for the reason that so many countries not only became involved, but for the first time in history combatants were drawn from all corners of the globe. It was an international confrontation, unparalleled in world history.

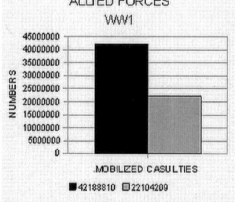

It was 'Great' on account of the number of dead, wounded and maimed bodies, from all walks of life and from all ages, reflecting starkly and without question the truthfulness of the Chinese proverb: 'War is death's feast'.

William Maylam waxes enthusiastically in his poem about the universality of WW2.

THE DIARY AND WRITINGS OF W A MAYLAM

CONSCRIPTED INTO THE ARMY IN WW II ON NOVEMBER 14TH 1940

BILL WAS TAKEN AWAY FROM HIS WIFE DOROTHY AND FOUR

CHILDREN -   WILLIAM AGED 8   +++   HAZEL AGED 6
             PETER   AGED 4   +++   EDNA AGED 6 MONTHS

THESE ARE HIS THOUGHTS AND WRITINGS WHILE SERVING IN THE

NORTH AFRICAN CAMPAIGN OF THE 8TH ARMY

HE NEVER SPOKE ABOUT THEM MUCH AFTER THE WAR

George Korankye

In Step

The Freedom armies march in step
Though far apart their ways may lie
Men of every creed and colour
Men prepared to fight and die
Moving in the same direction
With the same song in their soul

Brothers in a single purpose
Eyes upon a common goal
They have heard a bugle calling
And the throbbing of a drum
From the world's far distant corners
Free men marching see they come

That is not all the Great War did. It made people, for the first time, question their beliefs in an omnipotent God. The total of dead, wounded, maimed and 'physiologically lifeless' people made many to honestly and uniquely question the purpose of life. It started an exodus from the churches, which is still continuing in the 21st century.

Since the various established faiths could not offer acceptable reasons for the carnage unfolding before them, humans looked for an explanation elsewhere. And where did some find their answers?

Well, just before the Great War, Charles Darwin (1809-1882) brought forward his ideology of natural selection or, as it was explained to the ordinary man in the street, 'the theory of the survival of the fittest'. The Great War proved this hypothesis right. Adolph Hitler and his Nazi party, in pursuit of a 'master race' which weeded out the 'weak and undesirables', was to develop this suggestion into a 'working model'. He took the skeletal frames of this philosophy, put flesh onto it and gave it life by making blood run through this new proposition. This idea, which transformed into a guiding principle of the Nazi party, bred the 'blond hair, blue eyes' theory that would later give birth to what became known as the Holocaust.

The UK won her military campaigns, many believed not because of prayers to an Almighty God but to a new god that man found. This god was the god of Science.

The words of Epicurus, the ancient Greek philosopher (341-270 BC), 'It is folly for a man to pray to the gods for that which he has power to obtain by himself' became a swan song. It was science which many came to believe was responsible for the Allies' victory and not prayers.

There were those who still possessed some belief, but even those on the front line placed their real trust in the bullets that science had helped man to develop, not in an all-loving and caring God. A popular saying came about because of this ideology. It was: 'Praise the Lord but pass the ammunition'.

This is how William Maylam, a 'Desert Rat', felt, and those words appear at the end of his poem below.

Bang up to date a true story

The children at the Sunday school
Were paying scant attention
The teacher, quick to sense their mood
Applied an old invention
She said 'come now and listen to this
Each child will sing a hymn tune
And who sings best will win a prize
Some sweets will be their fortune'.

There followed many lovely hymns
Well known through the ages
As each child sang with lusty voice
In fits and starts and stages.
Then little Margaret four years old
Upset the competition
She sang with gust 'Praise the Lord
And pass the ammunition'.

Had not science given man the technology to develop a defensive 'shield' to the enemies' insidious gas attacks by inventing the gas mask during WW1 from scratch?

Had not the technology available to man at that time shaped the machine guns capable of firing hundreds of rounds a minute?

Scientific skills had created the aeroplane from a clumsy contraption designed by the Wright brothers, Orville (1871-1948) and Wilbur (1867-1912). From something which could only stay in the air for more than a few seconds was created a machine which was now capable of rivalling a bird, staying for hours in the air and reaping havoc on the enemy's positions.

The application of scientific knowledge had produced the tank, which became a 'saviour' for the British in the Battle of Cambrai in 1917. The tank had first appeared in the battle of the Somme (1916). The Germans were later to develop the tank further in the Second World War (1939-1945) and produce the dreaded 'Panzer'.

Yes, it was science developed by man that many believed had enabled the 'fittest to survive' and not God. The Second World War which followed the Great War showed that the term 'Great' was a misnomer. It was in fact a pygmy 'crossing of swords', because the Second World War surpassed it. In addition, it went on to demonstrate, on a far grander scale than previous battles, how science can become 'man's saviour' once again.

Radar, sonar and eventually the atom bomb all originated from the application of scientific knowledge. The legacy of the Atom bomb is still with us. It has even left its footprints in the art world. How?

In an article appearing in *The Art Newspaper* stated, under bold headlines, 'New hurdle for art forgers as A-bomb fallout is used to identify the fakes'. The article goes on to relate how the nuclear explosions carried out from the prototype stages of the Manhattan project until the eventual moratorium in 1966 released two very distinctive types of radioactive materials into the atmosphere. These materials were then absorbed by organic matters, such as plants. Any paintings using plant-derived binding agents will carry this as a footprint. This means that any pre WW2 painting that has been forged can be classified as fake, depending on whether it has the special radioactive material or not.[28]

The legacy of WW2 has found a useful purpose in, of all places, art.

The Great War also started an exodus from religious convictions and a move towards a more secular society. According to a survey conducted by *The Times* and

---

[28] *The Times* newspaper dated 31 May 2008, page 5, 'New hurdle for art forgers as A-bomb fallout is used to identify the fakes'. The article describes the two specific radioactive materials released from approximately 550 nuclear explosions from July 1945-1963 as isotopes, caesium-137 and strontium-90. It then goes on to say: 'Any work of art purporting to be more than 63 years old that registers trace amounts of the two isotopes can therefore be definitively declared a fake'. It goes on to say: 'Andrei Krusanov, a geochemist and art historian who has written books on the Russian avant-garde, said: "There cannot be any other way around it. Any oil painting made in the nuclear era will show traces of caesium-137 and strontium-90".'

reported in its 8 May 2008 edition, many people now believe that the UK is no longer a 'Christian' country and that churchgoing does not take precedence in their lives.[29]

Why? Because many 'experts' feel that religious dogma no longer has the same hold, nor does it have the same kudos or respect that it had before WW1. It has been relegated to a minor league as far as people are concerned.[30]

Of course, as with any survey or statistics, many disagreed and said the interpretations were flawed and left out alternative explanations for the decline in church attendance.

A poem written in 2007 by Darryl Ashton[31] demonstrates the attitude prevailing today:

The Modern Ten Commandments

God: 'What are you doing with the tablets of stone with My Ten Commandments? I thought I told you to take it down the mountain and to read it to the multitude?'

---

[29] 'Churchgoing on its knees as Christianity falls out of favour' by Ruth Gledhill, Religion Correspondent *The Times*, 8 May 2008.

[30] It is not the objective of this publication to enter into a religious debate. The cursory mention of religion is to provide the reader with changing attitudes since 1914 and to show that no aspect of human society/institution has been exempt from these upheavals. Shake-ups have affected economies, governments, businesses etc.

[31] Darryl is a prolific poet. He sent a vast collection of poems to the author. Unfortunately, most of them were unsuitable for the book. Nevertheless his wit and sarcasms are praiseworthy. He has had many poems printed in various newspapers and has won prizes for his works. He deals with all forms of modern day topics. Darryl has been advised to collate his poems into a book. He is currently looking at the feasibility of such a task.

Moses: 'Yes, you did, God, but I need to talk to you about that.'

God: 'What's to talk about? It was a simple enough task!'

Moses: 'That's what I thought, until the Health and Safety (H&S) spotted me trying to carry the tablets.'

God: 'What have they got to do with it?'

Moses: 'Well, God, they reckoned that it was either going to do my back in, might drop it on my foot, or somebody else's foot. Anyway, H&S weren't having it. I had to fill in a risk assessment form first.'

God: 'Anything else?'

Moses: 'As a matter of fact, there is. It was then the Politically Correct (PC) brigade got involved. Said the title was too abrupt. Didn't leave any room for negotiation.'

God: 'That was the idea. They are MY commands, that is why they are called Commandments. The title stays.'

Moses: 'Right, God, but there was a couple of other things they weren't happy about.'

God: 'What else were they moaning about?'

Moses: 'Well they didn't care for that bit about not worshipping any other Gods. Said it was discriminatory and might upset other religions.'

God: 'Anything else?'

Moses: 'The bit about honouring your father and mother. They reckon in single-parent families some of the kids don't know who their father is. Sometimes mother hasn't got a clue.'

God: 'Go on, let's have it all.'

Moses: 'The ad people and politicians are dead against the word "lie" - they say it is too judgmental. They prefer the phrases such as "putting a spin on it", or "presenting it in a better light", or "in the public interest".'

God: 'They are still liars, though.'

Moses: 'Oh yes, God, they lie for a living.'

God: 'Are there any of My Commandments these various meddlers are happy about?'

Moses: 'Well, God, they're OK with "You must not murder". And the one about stealing, although the politicians rob the people blind, but as they call it taxing, it's all right. Of course, the big stores don't agree with keeping the Sabbath special.'

God: 'I've a good mind to send down a plague of frogs to teach these sinners a lesson.'

Moses: 'No God, don't do that or we'll have the animal rights crowd all over us like a rash.'

Does this mean that belief in God is non existent? The surprising answer is no! Time and time again, many will profess a belief in God but will be against what they call 'organised religion'.

This belief in a powerful Being affects all classes, sexes, races and professions, including scientists, an occupation which one would think has no interest whatsoever in God in the modern era.

The conversion of ex-prime minister of the UK, Tony Blair, to Catholicism in 2007 is a case in point. Whilst in office he dismissed any questions about his beliefs. The rationale given by Alistair Campbell was: 'We don't do God in politics'.

A survey published by the Templeton Foundation in 2008 and discussed in *The Times* newspaper revealed 40 per cent of scientists purported a belief in God. However, this did not mean that God is consulted over every decision they make.

The churches have not taken this lying down and have also responded by informing the government that they are not pleased with the way they are being portrayed or ignored. In fact, they admit that Britain is moving ever closer to a secular society.[32]

The application of scientific knowledge in all areas of man's life has enabled man to build bigger, better as well as more accurate weapons of destruction. It helps mankind plan for the future by applying the principles of economics, predict and tract the pattern of epidemics with the discipline of epidemiology, explore space with the study of astronomy, probe the brain's functions in the field of neurology assisted by psychology, learn the workings of the body in the form of physiology, map the seas by oceanology, build superior buildings, ships and aeroplanes with engineering as the guiding principle.

Finally, with the help of archaeology, it has even enabled man to bring the past back to life. Science now shapes man's thinking in the present day more than any religious doctrine before the Great War. By way of proof, is it not true that any idea, philosophy or even medicines that cannot be proven scientifically are usually scorned? There is no doubt about it, we now live in an age of 'science and technology'.

The Great War was thus a distinctive turning point in man's history but that is not all the Great War did. What else did it do? Why is it 'Great'?

It is also 'Great' in that it led to drastic changes in the way human society behaved and the attitudes it had about itself, and how it viewed and treated other people within

---

[32] 'Church attacks Labour for Betraying Christians', *The Times* 7 June 2008; 'Does science make belief in God Obsolete?' *The Times* 26 May 2008 and Essays published by the Templeton Foundation at www.templeton.org/belief

and outside its own borders. The influx of immigrants and the shifting attitudes towards women is a classic example of how the Great War affected people and their mindset.

The Great War not only led to the greatest British casualty figures in history - over one million in the Battle of the Somme alone (1916) - but it was followed in the Second World War by the greatest British retreat at Dunkirk in May 1940 which resulted in the evacuation of over 300,000 men.

It would seem impossible to find any humour associated with this dire event in British history; yet we do, with help from George McMillan from Perth, who relates what he calls the DUNKIRK EXCITEMENT:

'Muriel (my aunt) was sitting at home in Middlesbrough in 1940, worried sick because there was no news of her husband Jack in France. Meanwhile, Jack, a Royal Engineer sergeant who had been blowing up bridges behind the retreating British Army for days from deep inside Belgium, was so exhausted on reaching the beaches at Dunkirk that he had fallen asleep under a sand dune.

'He was so tired he was oblivious to the bombing, machine-gunning and shelling. When he woke up, an officer chivvied him down to a waiting boat and he was ferried to one of the last destroyers to leave Dunkirk, then across the channel and home.

'On arrival at Dover, he at once sent a telegram home. When Muriel saw the postman, she nearly fainted, thinking it was bad news.

'She was so elated when she learned that Jack was safe that she set off at once to see Jack's mother to bring her the good tidings. Not until she was on the bus did she realise she was still in her pinny and slippers and had no money. The conductor asked:

"Where to, missus?"

"Jack's safe! He's coming home!" she replied.

"Yes, yes," said the conductor, "but where do want to go?"

"Jack's mother's," Muriel replied. At that, the conductor gave up. How Muriel ever got to her destination, heaven only knows, but she made it and brought tears and laughter to an old woman's delighted face.'

Talking of Dunkirk, another soldier wrote about a joke that he heard whilst in the forces. He swears that this is true.

It was about the veteran comedian Arthur Askey (1900-1982) who was performing somewhere in Lancashire during the Second World War. He recollects that the place was an Army hospital. Anyway, to cut a long story short, he remembers after his performance, Arthur is reputed to have said in his broad Liverpudian accent, 'Oh, we don't want thanking.' When pressed as to why he refused to accept the generous applause bestowed upon him by his grateful patients, he replied modestly it was in appreciation for '…all those lads did for us at Dunkirk.'

The commandant of the hospital, putting his hands to his mouth, cleared his throat and replied, 'Dunkirk? None of this lot has been further than Blackpool. This is a VD hospital.'

You'd think you couldn't get funnier than that, wouldn't you? Well, you would be wrong. Think of the reverse of Dunkirk and what comes to mind? D-day or Normandy. Instead of retreating, the British Army was returning with vengeance in mind. You would think the soldiers would be filled with hatred and anger and be downright sombre.

For a moment ponder on this question. What was 'a plenty' at Normandy? There was sun, sea and sand. This was paradise if you were going on holiday. However, if you were struggling under a heavy pack scrambling from

landing crafts onto a beach under constant enemy fire from artillery, rifles and bombs, the sea may not be very welcome.

This is precisely what Sergeant-Major William Brown relates about his D-day landings in 1944:

'The water filled the gas trousers. We could feel it sloshing around inside and we stood on the beach, like idiots, in trousers full of water.'[33] [34]

Oh, if only Beadle was about or perhaps the TV programme 'You've Been Framed', William Brown would surely have picked up his £250 cheque courtesy of

---

33 *Lest We Forget: Forgotten Voices 1914-1945* by Max Arthur (2007) p201. Courtesy Random House Publishing.
34 Cartoon by Jordon Krawczyk.

ITV. However, the mind boggles if he had to phone in to claim for his prize. Would some BBC stooge already have won it or...

The Great War had shown how science, coupled with technology, could reap havoc on the enemy; however, it also gave birth to something else, a new sense of values or commitments called patriotism. Nationalism, which is loyalty to one's country of birth, irrespective of that country's actions, began a feeling which later led to the phrase 'my country right or wrong'.

Politicians saw this new force of patriotism as a binding agent to unite the general public behind any cause that it could promote as endangering the security of the nation.

This theme runs throughout speeches of politicians over the years. In his inaugural speech, President John F Kennedy of The United States of America said on Friday, 20 January 1961 '...And so, my fellow Americans: ask not what your country can do for you - ask what you can do for your country'.

As the possibility of disintegration stared politicians in the face, as the old world order was disappearing in front of their eyes, politicians saw nationalism as an answer to their prayers; this new 'superglue' would hold the nation 'through thick and thin'.

Former Professor of Modern History at Oxford University, Sir Michael Howard in the book 'Oxford History of The Twentieth Century', postulates that nationalism was the antidote to fragmentation, the breaking up of an empire.

The causes of war are many and varied and it is beyond the scope of this book to discuss this aspect in detail. It would be fair to say that the threat of losing its national identity was a great motivator in uniting the whole nation in the First and Second World wars.

Very few people dared to question a government's actions if that regime was seen to be protecting the nation's national identity. Both 'combatants and aggressors', both 'friends and foes', all appealed to the people's nationalistic feelings and it worked. It hit a nerve in each nation because, had it not been a winning formula, there would have been nothing 'Great' about WW1; it would have been just like any other war.

So successful was the generating of nationalistic feelings that Captain Anthony Rhodes of the Royal Engineers remembers clearly:

'One of the things we were told - the sort of rumour that was going round - was that the Germans couldn't possibly have built up an army since 1933, in six years. People even said that, when the Germans paraded their tanks through the cities of Northern Germany, some of them were made of cardboard. That is the sort of rumour one heard'.[35]

'The feeling of nationalism persists well into the 21st century. When it is mixed with a nation's real or perceived threat, that its culture is in danger of disappearing, or very soon it will cease to exist, it will pave the way for what President George Bush is alleged to have said in 2002: "No, I know all the war rhetoric, but it's all aimed at achieving peace".

'The words appear to mirror those of Aristotle, Greek Philosopher (384-322BC), quoted earlier who said: "We make war that we may live in peace".'

---

35 *Forgotten Voices of the Second World War: A new history of world war two in the words of the men and women who were there* by Max Arthur (2005) p19. Courtesy Random House Publishing.

Chapter 3

The Talent War Reveals

'Sharing and giving are the ways of God'
Proverb of the Sauk American Indian Tribe

During wars the competence (and incompetence) of generals becomes so clear that even a blind man could see what was going on. The decisions that politicians, who some people feel are either not aware of, or choose to ignore the sufferings of, the ordinary man on the street becomes a talking point. In fact many come to feel that the politicians and at times the generals commanding the armed forces do not actually have 'a scobbie' or an in-depth understanding of the sacrifices that they are calling on the people to make. Oh! They may wax lyrically about food shortages and the need to tighten belts, but you can 'bet your last dollar' that they will still be able to have their luxuries.

Others feel differently and they will give examples of how an important person responded to their needs or plea for help. This is part of letter sent by Mrs Stuart of Buxton:

'When my husband was in Burma with the Gurkhas, Lord Louis Mountbatten, Commander of the S E Asia Operation, arrived to give a morale-boosting talk to the troops, who were lined up in a square. At the end he asked if there was anything they wanted. A shout came from one of the British companies, "Some Easter eggs!"

79

Sure enough, on Easter Sunday a plane flew over and dropped a mass of small pink Easter eggs.'

Can you now understand why in such a climate everyone becomes an authority on war issues? Some people will say with deep feeling and enthusiasm that the war is moral and that they have to take part. Others will take an opposite view and believe that if they refuse any kind of military service they will be called 'conscies' or conscientious objectors. Everyone will definitely have an opinion and a solution.

What do you think of this solution by Herbert (1890-1971)[36] who suggested that, instead of dropping bombs on the Germans, a novel idea be tried out using a play on Hitler's *Mein Kampf.* He said that Britain should leaflet the Germans, or 'Mein Pamphf' them. This 'Mein Bombf' campaign would have got the desired result.

What a brilliant idea. But suppose this brilliant idea did not work - what should be done? Herbert gives additional suggestions that if 'Mein Bombf' was unsuccessful then Britain should release its secret weapon. This weapon would be so devastating it would bring the Germans to their knees in a short period of time. There would be no need to drop incendiary bombs on the poor Germans, no carpet bombing of their beloved cities like Cologne or Dresden with high explosives, no need to send time delayed bombs on parachutes. The Germans would then not have started bombing Britain's cities. In fact, the war could be completed averted because the Germans would all be bogged down by this secret weapon. What was this dreaded secret weapon?

---

36 *I couldn't Help Laughing: An anthology of wartime humour* ed DB Wyndham (1940). Out of print.

Die Laughing – War Humour

Well, the British liked a good ol' custard pie fight. Watch any silent movie and you can rest assured that there will be a custard pie fight. We seem to love this quaint British trait. Herbert reckons the war could be won by dropping custard pies on the Germans and really messing things up - pardon the pun. Just think of the mess of cleaning up the remains of millions of custards dropped from a great height; if that did not work, why not drop nuts on them? That would really make them 'nutty'.

There would be no need to fight them on the beaches, in the air, on the sea or on the land - in fact, there would be no need to fight them at all. What a brilliant idea! Why, oh why, did these politicians not think of this as part of their bombing strategies? The author commissioned a new unknown artist to illustrate the scene below. Is this Britain's latest talented cartoonist?[37]

37 Cartoon by Jordon Krawczyk.

Straight away you can see that out of the woodwork come the experts, who will be able to put their own interpretations on the events unfolding day by day. These professionals will become 'cannon fodder' for the humorists.

Beachcomber[38], another humorist during WW2, penned a rather comical view of the so called 'Experts'. He said:

'My favourite character nowadays is either "Government spokesman" or "leading authority". I am not sure which.

"Leading authority" scored very heavily the other day. He "Declared that the figures of civilians killed in recent raids are small compared with the total civil population or with the losses of the fighting services in this or the last was."

'To reach that startling conclusion it is necessary to be a leading authority. No ordinary person would ever suspect such a thing.

"Government spokesman" is usually the man who is reported as having said that unless Hitler's invasion comes some time or other, it will probably not come at all. He also says that if the Germans ever became short of petrol it cannot fail to affect their planes and their mechanized forces.

'Then there is a "High official" who says that "there are only two alternatives before the Italians - to attack or not to attack."

'There are also "Government circles". It is always "being said in Government circles" that Hitler would prefer a short, successful war to a long unsuccessful one.

---

[38] Beachcomber courtesy Express Newspapers

'Victory is his object rather than defeat. It is only by obtaining the victory that he can win. If, on the other hand, he is defeated, then he will lose the war.

'Let us not forget "Medical expert", who has recently discovered that lack of sleep increases fatigue, and that the more you worry, the more your nerves will be affected.

'Strap me! How lucky we all are to be so surrounded, hedged in and propped up by so many cohorts of brilliant chatterboxes.'

This kind of environment therefore proves a fertile ground for 'funny sayings' and drawings for all the warring parties. No one is exempt, even children get in on the act. William Moore (1934-), who lived in Tasburgh when he was a snippet of a lad during WW2, tells in a humorous way how a child saw things. He says:

'During the German raids the shed where we kept our cycles was hit by tracer bullets. That's the only damage we had. The effect of bombing on Norwich was felt even at this distance of nine miles away. Our bedroom floors were not level so we had various size wood blocks under the furniture. When bombs made impact the bed, for instance, would jump from the blocks and one leg or another would miss the block on return. This was a cast iron double bed, so it's impossible to describe what a direct hit must have been like.

'Towards the end of the war, "doodlebugs" (German pilotless rocket planes) went over our house. It was a direct path with a timed destination before it would explode. The doodlebug had a green light showing; when this light went out it meant in two minutes it would crash to earth and explode.

George Korankye

'One summer evening, one doodlebug whisked over the house, a second followed but the light went out in the distance before reaching us. It came very low, passed over in about half a minute, and exploded in a field about two miles away. The impact lifted me off my feet; I shrieked and ran to my grandmother.'

By their drawings, children demonstrate they too are fully aware of what is going on.[39]

This is some World War II graffiti found in the underground air raid shelter at Sutton High School and also the shrub verge at Lower Street, both Plymouth. Done by schoolchildren from primary to grammar age, they are of Hitler, Churchill, Goring and Mussolini and they give a stunning window into the past.[40]

Politicians on both sides of a conflict will also see the power of illustrations. Kitchener's 'Your Country Needs You' is now an iconic image, instantly recognised worldwide. And what is the result? My! It has spawned many imitations throughout the 20th century.

---

39 Courtesy www.cyberheritage.org.

40 'Cyberheritage' delivers history in the form of text and photographs onto your desktop. Material covered is varied. Many photographs are high quality allowing a user to download them and print them out for inclusion in such things as school projects. Currently there are over 12,000 photos spread across all the 130 plus web sites.

Die Laughing – War Humour

Yes, editors find that in times of war they have at their disposal an arsenal of weapons to use. These 'armaments' are cartoons, illustrations, satires, and biting sarcasm. They can be just as deadly as any modern day missile and as accurate as any laser guided bomb. These 'weapons of war' can also be fired so accurately that people can see the futility of a war a country is engaging in.

Like arrows, graphics can be aimed accurately at editors' readers if he/she wants to commend acts of bravery, not just on the front line where the 'lads' are dying, but also on the home front where the people are tightening their belts.

Serious issues can be discussed openly and thought provoking questions can be asked without appearing disloyal to the nation's cause by the use of carefully worded sayings.

On the other hand, those who know that their life could be snuffed out at any time face the situation with, at times, unbelievable hilarity.

To put their loved ones at ease, these individuals far away in ever changing climates will at times try to show the funny side of a traumatic situation they are experiencing.

Take a look at this poem by William Maylam:

Waiting for a letter - how long the time can be
Looking for the postman - waiting anxiously
Many wives and mothers just live from day to day
Hoping for a letter - a little line to say
'All's well,' for that's sufficient
When loved ones are apart
To banish fear and worry away
And cheer the lonely heart.

As can be seen from the poem, an unintentional side effect of any war is the discovery of talents previously unknown to the nation. Soldiers (this term is used to represent all the armed forces) become poets overnight as they wax lyrically of their loved ones left back at home; some become cartoonists or illustrators, questioning their superiors' behaviour with their stark images.

They 'fire their weapons of war' as accurate as a sniper's bullet. They hit the mark with just as deadly a force as a projectile from a rifle, making people either think about the current conflict, or comfort their loved ones left behind who are 'keeping the home fires burning'.

Bathing was of course a luxury in the theatre of war. You could not just go upstairs, turn the tap on and get hot flowing water. Nor could you laze about in a candlelit bathroom with the sweet aroma of scented candles wafting in your nostrils. Absent, also, would be the sound of a gramophone - no stereos, tapes, CDs, ipods or MP3 players - with its soothing music as you listened to the hypnotic sounds of water flowing gently into the bath.

Of course, during WW1 there were no combi boilers - hot water came from coal fires fitted with back boilers. Many baths were either community ones or, if you were lucky, you got your weekly wash in the tub at home.

Electric immersion heaters appeared later with the famous gas 'Ascot boilers', which made hot water possible for a few more. So the lack of personal hygiene must have troubled a few. Some will remember the Lifebuoy advert 'get a kick out of life and kick out BO'. Well, many must have been self-conscience of their 'pong'.

Once again, some Smart Alec called Peter Stegall decided to have a joke on his mates. He relates:

'Early in March 1945 the regiment arrived in Marseilles, having sailed from Alexandria in Egypt. After a night or two in a tented camp, we boarded a train of box wagons labelled "Dix chevaux ou quarante hommes" (10 horses or 40 men) and headed up the Rhone valley. Somewhere on the way north we stopped for a while in open country. Having walked along the track to the front of the train and back, I told some of my fellow "hommes" on our box wagon that there was a shower in the front carriage. Several of them grabbed soap and towels and hopefully hurried forward. They were disappointed to find that the front carriages contained comfortable accommodation for officers. Fortunately for me my colleagues took it all as a joke.'

Very interesting, eh? Special accommodation for the officers? It would appear that the officers' carriages were 'home from home', an interesting insight into life at the time for the ordinary 'squaddie'.

As can be readily seen by just a few of these incidents, a consequence of war is that it proves to be a fertile ground for hilarity. In the midst of destruction, decadence and sheer brutality, a whole nation finds that it can laugh not only at itself but at what it sees as the enemy.

In fact, cast your mind back to Dunkirk, which has been immortalised in the minds of the British public. Imagine awaiting evacuation and being under constant fire. The proud British Army which controlled an empire in which it was once said 'the sun never set upon' was now in retreat.

How depressing it must have been for the men. It is well known that the spirit of an army can affect its morale. A case in point is the three hundred Spartans who were able to inflict a memorable defeat on the mighty empire of its time. They proved true the Arabian proverb: 'An army of sheep led by a lion would defeat an army of lions led by a sheep'.[41]

The story told by Dickie about an incident involving Major Richard Bisgood on La Panne Beach, north east of Dunkirk, is unbelievable. Read on and see if you agree:

'Parts of the 206\52 anti-tank regiment have joined many other units on the beaches awaiting evacuation. Fairly constant air raids, mostly by Stuka dive bombers, are taking place up and down the beach. There is also a steady delivery of German artillery shells exploding among the countless vehicles and other debris covering the sand. The order has been given to the troops to dig in among the sand dunes until it's their turn to join the columns of men stretching out into the sea.

'It was my uncle, Frank Bisgood, who at length explained the Oak Leaf (a mention in despatches) on my father's medal ribbons. Characteristically, Dickie, my father, wasn't intent on blowing his own trumpet, no matter how many times his son pestered him. He saw the whole incident as a bit of lunacy on his part and was surprised that such a fuss should be made of it.

'Having endured the continuous bombardment for four days, an increasing number of troops on the beach were becoming severely shell shocked. On occasion, a man would break from cover in an attempt to run from

---

41 In the historic Battle of Thermopylae (480 BC) which was later portrayed in two films both entitled 300 Spartans (1962 and 2007). A 300 small band of Greek soldiers held back a vastly superior Persian force led by King Xerxes I of Persia. Although they were finally defeated, this courageous last stand, later to be used in connection with General Custer (Custer's Last Stand), contributed to the final demise of the mighty Persian Empire.

the exploding ordnance around them. Whilst dug into the sand, they stood some chance of survival as many low flying shell splinters were smothered by the sand. On their feet, out in the open, the possibility of injury or death was all too high.

'In order to restore calm, Dickie fetched his shaving gear and wandered down to the water's edge. He took off his steel helmet and proceeded to attempt to lather up his face. Every time a bomb burst nearby he flinched and more often than not nicked his skin. There was great hilarity among the men, and many of those who had been close to breaking were reassured and calmed by the ridiculous sight of an officer busily sticking bits of newspaper to the cuts on his face.'[42]

When we think of war poets, Siegfried Sassoon (1886-1967), Wilfred Owen (1893-1918) or even Rupert Brooke (1887-1915) and their like are remembered. But there were ordinary men and women whose wit and sarcasms were just as powerful. This book has examples of real men and women from all walks of life who relate at times in a funny way their experiences.

William Maylam's poem about sincerity is thought provoking:

Sweet is the sound and sweet the meaning of sincerity
Without it there can be no faith
No friendship and no sympathy
In the firm clasp of the hands we feel it
In the clear eye its light we see
For here hearts speak and understand
The language of sincerity

---

42 Dickie, WW2 The People's War. Courtesy BBC.

Now, at first glance there appears nothing brilliant about those words, but on reflection would you say that there is an element of truth? He is no great Greek or Roman philosopher, he does not possess pearls of wisdom quoted by learned men. Nevertheless, in a few words, he has succinctly shown the value of sincerity. This quality, according to him, is essential for all true friendships, faiths and even true love.

You can be sincere and still be wrong, nevertheless there are elements of truth in his words. The point is, had Mr Maylam not been put in that unenviable position of seeing death and destruction on a daily basis, experiencing a helping hand from complete strangers, would he have otherwise found the inspiration to write such thought provoking words?

Another consequence of war is that it brings people, whose paths may never have crossed, together. William Moore (1934 -) by sheer coincidence met the Hollywood actor James Stewart:

'Around 1943, when the Americans were based in the Norfolk area, many from Hethel would use the local pubs. Beer was being rationed and pubs were only open Friday, Saturday and Sunday.

'The Americans would drink the nearest pub dry on a Friday and carry on through the local villages. This is how our family entertained James Stewart for approximately six weeks for Sunday lunch.

'James Stewart, his second in command, plus staff sergeant/batman-come-bodyguard were cycling past our cottage to the West End public house at Saxlingham Thorpe one Sunday morning. One of the three got a puncture. They had no idea how to mend it nor had any tools to do so. They spotted me (aged 9) by my gate and asked if anyone could help. I knew that my father could do the job even if I could not and the three left their cycles.

'They returned about 2:15pm and knocked at the front door. My grandma answered. The aroma of Sunday lunch roast beef was apparent, whereupon my grandmother invited the gentlemen to lunch with us. They were most delighted so we had sweets, oranges and tinned fruit, etc for six weeks.

'I was given a £5 note for mending the puncture. My father took care of this. It was more than his weekly wage.

'James Stewart was sent from Tibenham, his command base, to Hethel for this short period "incognito" with the other two gents. I only knew this by turning the bike upside down and out dropped numerous items, including his dog tags.

'I still did not realise he was famous, so the name meant nothing. I still have a photo taken by the staff sergeant of my grandparents at the cottage door (it was illegal for members of the public to use a camera in wartime).

'The master sergeant, a gunner, was later killed on a mission.'

Yes, war affects the fabric of society. However, WW1 created changes so dramatic that it has been said that the world has not fully recovered.

In the midst of all the carnage that war brings, people look for an outlet for their guilt, fears, pent-up feelings, sorrows and, yes, even their hatred.

All these feelings thus find an outlet in humour in all its various forms and guises during times of war and certainly, no matter what profession you are, you are sure to find yourself being ridiculed.

Here follows a poignant poem by William Maylam:

<u>A Safe Return</u>

Many things I wish for you
As you go forth - I know not where
A good companion on the Journey
Health and luck and fortune four
But there's one prayer - one wish - one hope
That night and morning I renew
A speedy and a safe return
This, Dear, is my wish for you

The thoughts of William Maylam above were the thoughts of many millions on both sides of the war. Several thousands will have their wishes granted, an untold number not. A number will receive their loved ones back, but not in the way that they left. And yet millions still managed a smile at home and on the front.

It never ceases to amaze me how much cartoon talent the war produced. On the following page is one sent to the author by Anne Bagette from her First World War scrapbook. The artist, no doubt, captures the moment.

The date is 1915. The soldier has just returned from a gruelling tour of duty. He has missed his dearly beloved and is looking forward to rekindling his love.

On the scene appears a Charlie Chaplin look-alike. Straightaway it conjures up a scene of frustration for the soldier.

Does your heart no go out to him and his beloved? Here he is, deprived of the love of his 'one and only' for goodness knows how long. All he's been used to are rats,

"CIRCUMSTANCES~

~ALTER~

~FACES.

A Study in expressions.

Birmingham.
X. mas Day 1915

mud and gas. All this, mixed in with the body odour of thousands of unwashed men and the decaying flesh of men and beasts - no wonder he has a smile on his face. This serene scene is altered by a 'change in circumstances'.

93

On reflection, is that not true of many of life's problems? We may have a routine all planned out, but then time and unforeseen circumstances alter these plans. Looking at things from the point of view of these soldiers, the war definitely altered many lives.

Another gift from Anne Bagette is a fusilier soldier's thoughts on his daily routine:

The Daily Routine of a soldier

6.30am Reveille-Christians Awake (A/M 61)*
6.45 Rouse Parade - Art thou weary art thou languid (A/M 254)*
7.00 Breakfast - Meekly wait and murmur not
8.15 Company Parade - When he cometh
8.45 Manoeuvres - Fight the good fight (A/M 540)*
11.45 Swedish Drill - Here we suffer grief and pain
1.00pm Dinner - Come ye thankful people come (A/M382)*
2.15 Rifle Drill - Go labour on (Hymn B 415)*
3.15 Lectures by Officers - Abide with me (A/M 27)*
4.20 Dismiss - Praise God from whom all blessings flow
5.00 Tea - What means this eager anxious throng
6.00 Free for Night - O lord how happy shall we be (A/M 276*
6.20 Out Of Bounds - We may not know we cannot tell. (A/M 332)*
10.00 Last Post - All are safely gathered in (A/M 382)*
10.15 Lights Out - Peace perfect peace (A/M 27)*
10.30 Inspection by Guards- Sleep on Beloved

*In her letter Anne Baggett says:

94

'These poems and the cartoons were in an autograph book that belonged to my mother-in-law and came into

The Daily Routine of a Soldier's Life.

Time	Event	Hymn
6-30 A.M.	Reveille	Christians Awake
6-45	Rouse Parade	Art thou weary Art thou languid
7-0	Breakfast	Meekly wait & murmur not
8-15	Coy Parade	When he cometh
8-45	Manoeuvres	Fight the good fight
11-45	Swedish Drill	Here we suffer grief & pain
1-0 P.M.	Dinner	Come ye thankful people come
2-15	Rifle Drill	Go labour on
3-15	Lectures by Officers	Abide with me
4-20	Dismiss	Praise God from whom all blessings flow
5-0	Tea	What means this eager anxious throng
6-0	Free for night	O Lord how happy shall we be
6-20	Out of bounds	We may not know we cannot tell
10-0	Last post	All are safely gathered in
10-15	Lights out	Peace perfect Peace
10-30	Inspection by Guard	Sleep on Beloved

Fusiliers. 1916.

our possession when she died. As a young woman she worked in Oxford during the First World War, and she often visited the wounded soldiers, who were in Oxford colleges, which were being used as hospitals.

'She would take them gifts and we presume she would have asked them to write in her autograph book, so I don't have any information on who they were or where they came from.

'The poem of *The Daily Routine* is certainly made up from hymns. I have looked through the Ancient and

Modern Book, also the Methodist Hymn book and have been able to find some but not all of them. The Hymn book I took these numbers from is dated 1938 so there may not be the same in a more modern one.'

Relaying more wartime experiences, Trevor Minns from Kent writes to the author:

'I recently read your letter in the local paper asking if there was any evidence of wartime humour... This got me thinking. In some memorabilia left by my wife's grandmother I remember seeing some old postcards (see colour image pages) from her husband. He was a regular and served in France. After a search among the artefacts I located the cards I had remembered...'

'...Old contemptible Sergeant John Alexander Pryke (Alex) died in 1964 at the age of just 73. His army career began at the beginning of the 20th century. He was dissatisfied with the butcher boy job, after his employer was swallowed up by a larger organisation, leaving him unemployed. He turned, like so many others, to a life as a regular soldier, joining up on 10 April 1908. With his initial training completed he was stationed at Gosport. He trained as a signaller and was assigned to the 5th Siege Battery RGA. It was while he was in Gosport that he met his future wife, who was in service as a maid.

'At the outbreak of war Alex was sent to France where he served for the entire war on different fronts. As we all realise now, life was tough, and to get through such atrocities the soldier looked upon war as a "game". This was illustrated through an extract from journals found in Alex's wife's possessions.

'In his spare time, Alex was always thinking of home, and the loved ones that he had been separated from. All correspondence was censored but the message was always of a cheery nature. At the beginning plain cards were the standard issue.'

Although Alex survived the war, he had his fair share of near misses. This extract was taken from his daughter's journals:

'Alex was twice recommended for the Military Medal for "conspicuous Bravery" but his commanding officer refused to forward his name, saying that his men knew how to do their duty without bits of putty.

'The closest escape he had was a bullet through his telephone, which he was carrying under his arm!'

Alex's second daughter's son has the very bullet as a keepsake.

Note the drawing, above, by one of the soldiers. On the following page, is an old postcard from WW2, which he, Alex, sent from India.

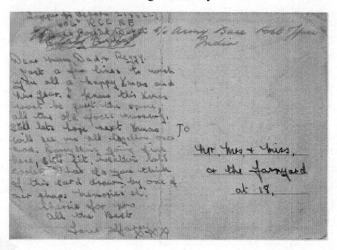

The image above is thought provoking. The next chapter contains an image that has stood the test of time.

Chapter 4

The Enduring Power of an Image

'The release of atom power has changed everything
except our way of thinking... If only I had known, I
should have become a watchmaker'

Albert Einstein

If you were to pick up any history book 'worth its salt' or
lucky enough to have a chat with a few professors of
history, you will find that they will all agree that 1914
was a turning point in human history. One era closed and
a new chapter in human history began. How did the
general population view the calamities that lay ahead?
Would the nations have embraced war so cheerfully if the
final figures of dead and wounded had been published in
advance?

There is a well known saying 'there are no mistakes
with hindsight'. However, even with hindsight, could the
politicians, businessmen, religious leaders - these so-
called 'defenders of the nation' - have averted this
catastrophe?

Some people actually believe that had the powers that
be foreseen the tragedies, perhaps they could have come
up with a solution. In fact, quite a number think that the
war could have been averted. The war, it has been said,
was the first 'popular war' to be fought by the United
Kingdom. The power of the media was put to its full use.
Never before had a whole nation wholeheartedly

George Korankye

embraced a conflict that was to inflict such misery upon it.

Have you seen Kitchener's (1850-1916) famous image?[42] Would you say that it has an unforgettable impact on you? This is an example of how a powerful illustration can be used to recruit people in their thousands. In fact, so memorable and powerful is this image that it is still recognisable today, worldwide. People talk about the Battle of the Somme (1916), arguably one of the bloodiest battles in the history of the UK, or the Battle of Passchendaele (1917). Incidentally, historians at times refer to it as the Third Battle of Ypres or to Third Ypres. This was one of the major battles of the Great War.

The battle that has become synonymous with slaughter must surely be Verdun (1916). Many people will recollect Czar Nicholas II (1868-1918) and the overthrow of the royal family in Imperial Russia during the Russian Revolution of 1917. But if we are honest, you have to be of a certain age to remember the above incidents. For these events to have affected you and then go that step further and leave an 'imprint' on your mind, you either must be a student of history, some of these incidents must have touched you personally, or someone you love must have been affected by these things and then related these episodes to you.

But there is a picture that every generation will instantly recognise, an image that has what is called the 'wow' factor. Do you know what it is? It is an aspect of the Great War that many people forget. One 'Great' graphic image that this period in history produced was Kitchener's 'Your Country Needs You'.

---

42 http://en.wikipedia.org/wiki/Lord_Kitchener_Wants_You

BRITONS

"WANTS YOU"

JOIN YOUR COUNTRY'S ARMY!
GOD SAVE THE KING

The Kitchener illustration (above) has spawned many copycat versions (see colour pages). The method of a hand pointing directly at the viewer and apparently following as the viewer moves round has inspired several imitations.

How successful was this image? Well, it is claimed that it resulted in thousands embracing this new conflict against what they saw as the battle between the forces of 'evil'. This was a righteous war as far the general population was concerned against a barbarian: this opponent would treat his foes, even children, mercilessly.

In fact, so successful was 'Kitchener's' image that everybody and his granny wanted to enrol.

Talking of images, the story of Bill's father comes to mind. His father served on *HMS Kepel*, a destroyer in the Royal Navy, from 1939-1945. Bill's primary reason for wishing his father's experiences to be related was the hope of leaving a permanent tribute to his father in print. He recollects a time when his father's ship:[43]

'…was due royal inspection/visit by, I believe, King George. My Dad was given the honour of breaking the Royal Standard as the king stepped on board ship.

'The officer that had delegated this task to my father had carefully written the instructions on what to do. So before the royal arrived, a white line had been painted on the quayside. The rule, I believe, is this: the royal standard can only fly in one place; it arrives with the king on the front of his car, and then the transfer is made as the flag is lowered on the car and then the same flag is broken on the ship's mast.

'Now, the thing is it cannot fly in two different places at the same time - if it does, whoever is responsible is on a mega charge, as it is a big disrespect to the crown. So here we are, my Dad has got his bit of paper that says: "When the king steps over the white line, then you break the Royal Ensign". The officer made sure my Dad understood the implications of getting it wrong, so he checked the note, yep no problem. So the king turned up,

43 'My father's name is William Henry Cleaver and the ship he served on was HMS Kepel. The captain of the ship was the subject of a famous legal case in which he was accused, in a badly written book, of deserting a convoy. He won major damages, which he donated to charity, as it was proved he left under orders. I think there was some link to the pursuit of the Bismarck when the Hood got sunk.'

everyone was there to great him in their best uniforms, my Dad is watching carefully for him to step over the line, breaks the ensign – job's a good one.

'Then the band strikes up the national anthem and the king takes a step backwards over the line.

'Result was 2 x flags flying. My father ended up in the brig. The officer came down to see him about charges. If he hadn't kept that piece of paper he would probably still have been there.'

Bill's request for his father to be remembered has been granted. He goes on to say how his father has left an indelible mark on his life. He remembers with fondness the love he showed him.

During WW1 the German soldier was portrayed as an 'infidel' or a 'Hun' without any mercy, as the illustration on the following page by *Punch* goes on to show. This was distressing to them.

Sergeant Stefan Westmann, a German soldier in 1914, recollects how during their advancements in the first phase of the war they came to a small village.

The villagers pleaded with them not to delimb their children. This was initially funny, but on quiet reflection he realised the power of propaganda. His laughter then turned to anger.[44]

Let's not forget that the same message was being relayed to those on the opposing side.

A publication that came to have 'clout' at the time of the two world wars was *Punch*. This magazine pulled 'no punches' in trying to get its message across to a wide audience.

44 *Lest We Forget: Forgotten Voices 1914-1945* by Max Arthur (2007) p31. Courtesy Random House Publishing.

George Korankye

Study of a German Gentleman going into Action
(Courtesy *Punch* September 1914)

Text: **God (and the women) our shield.**

There were a minority of voices who also foresaw its grave consequences. The cartoonist Dyson (1880-1938) it is said 'swore never to draw a line that didn't show war as 'the filthy business it is'.[45]

England's Millicent Garrett Fawcett and Scotland's Chrystal Macmillian of the International Suffrage Alliance, which was inaugurated in 1902 in The United States of America, sent this plea to the Foreign Office and to all the embassies of the 'opposing nations' based in London:

'We, the women of the world, view with apprehension and dismay the present situation in Europe, which

---

45 *World War II In Cartoons* (1989) by Mark Bryant p9.

threatens to involve one continent, if not the whole world, in the disasters and horrors of war…whatever its results the conflict will leave mankind the poorer. We appeal to you to…avert deluging half the civilized world in blood.'[46]

Mrs Fawcett's pleas fell on deaf ears and therefore, not wishing to harm her cause, encouraged her members to throw in their lot with the country's cause and help the war effort.

However, this was a 'popular war'. All these minority warnings fell on deaf ears. So powerful, so all embracing was the call to war, that even boys were 'telling fibs' so that they would be sent to the front line. Of course, the illustrators picked this up too.

Text: **OFFICER (to boy of thirteen who, in his effort**

to get taken on as a bugler, has given his age as sixteen): 'Do you know where boys go who tell lies?' APPLICANT: 'To the Front, sir.'

(Courtesy *Punch* August 1915)

You may well wonder why a little 'whipper snapper' of a lad would tell fibs to enlist. One reason may well be that the school leaving age at the time was 14. It was 'part and parcel' for young school children to go 'tattie picking' during the school holidays to supplement the

---

46 *Women At War* (2002) p17. Courtesy Imperial War Museum.

family's income. By the age of 16, many young men were physically fit and capable of heavy manual work.

George Glover recollects, as a 16-year-old during WW2, being employed at Plodder's shed as a cleaner. He states:

'...as a 16-year-old and crossing the main line from my parents' house, for the midnight cleaning shift (after a night out with my mates). I was surprised to see all the engines scattered all over the yard instead of stabled for the night. On looking on I was disheartened to learn that the 10.00pm coalman had gone AWOL (Absent Without Leave) and that I had to take his place and do my best to stop any delays...with heavy heart I approached the coal bench to commence an impossible task...but I GOT STUCK IN and SHOVELLED and SHOVELLED for ages (engine after engine) until, black with coal dust and sweat, I eventually coaled the last one, and went for my WELL EARNED scoff and brew, etc...to be laughed at as only the whites of my eyes were visible.'

Poor George must have looked like a raccoon. He goes on to say:

'With all the FIREDROPPING...ash loading and coal bench work as a youngster, I got muscles ON my MUSCLES... (My PARTY PIECE was to be able to LIFT anyone up on a SHOVEL'S BLADE)...and to such an extent that my own brother wouldn't let me tighten a nut or screw on his bike or whatever as I often sheared off the heads...but became useful in later life when attacked twice by armed robbers, whilst employed by the Royal Mail, and subdued them, although I'm known as a placid person normally.'

It can be seen that many youngsters, if they lied about their age, could easily con recruiting sergeants who were desperate to enlist as many men as possible for the war effort.

Mary Turner, who puts forward the view that the Suffragette leader Emily Pankhurst may have contributed to this, has suggested another reason why some youngsters enrolled. Shortly after the commencement of WW1, the suffragettes suspended their militancy. Emily Pankhurst then devoted her energies to drumming up support for the war against Germany. Recruiting men into the armed forces was, as far as she was concerned, one way of demonstrating how patriotic her organisation could be.

This zeal, however, had a downside. Mary Turner continues:

'A less savoury element of her effort was to encourage her supporters to give a white feather, denoting cowardice, to any young man who was not in uniform. Young men, sometimes too young to enlist, were "persuaded" to join up in this way.'[47]

In such a climate where white feathers were being routinely dished out and human nature being what it is, 'Murphy's law' will come into operation – 'what can go wrong will go wrong'. There were reported cases in which young male recruits on leave and therefore in civilian clothes were mistaken for 'draft dodgers', handed white feathers and marched to recruiting stations, only for the women to find out that they were drastically mistaken.

---

47 *The Women's Century: A Celebration of Changing Roles 1900-2000* by Mary Turner (2006) p 35. Courtesy National Archives.

George Korankye

Noonan relates the tale of Major Crozier[48] and Max Arthur gives the example of Private Norman Demuth, both during the First World War. In the latter's case the incident took place in a bus and, when the passengers found out that the woman in question was 'mistaken, she was well and truly barracked by the rest of the people. I sat back and laughed like mad'. Whilst in the former case the recruiting officers called the woman an 'interfering time wasting harridan'.[49]

Have you ever felt really embarrassed because you were mistaken about a certain situation or read too much into an incident? If you have you will sympathise with how these women felt. Imagine a whole busload of people not laughing with you but laughing at you!

No war is fought without armies. In the next chapter you will see what situations combatants faced and how they handled it.

48 *Tales From the Mess* by Miles Noonan (1983) p41.
49 *Forgotten Voices of The Great War:* by Max Arthur (2003) p170. Courtesy Random House publishing.

Chapter 5

The Armed Forces

'The human race has one really effective weapon, and
that is laughter'
Mark Twain[50] (1835-1910)

The armed forces of all the warring nations before the
Great War had been small professional bands, like most
armies of the 21st century. During previous wars these
'professionals' would go out into the field and 'square up
to one another'. The army that got the upper hand became
the victor and so won the right to impose its will on the
conquered. When it came to peace treaties, the champion
could either show leniency to the vanquished or it could
impose so great a punishment on its rival that its
opponent would find it hard to wage another war.

Many historians agree that the punitive terms of the
Treaty of Versailles (1919), which brought the Great War
to an end, actually sowed the seeds for the next 'Great'
war. The terms were so harsh for Germany that it was in
effect brought to its knees as it struggled to pay
compensation for the troubles the allies said it had
caused.

As far as the victors were concerned, this upstart of a
challenger had dared to challenge the mighty British

---

[50] Mark Twain was a prolific American author and humorist. His
books include 'The Adventures of Huckleberry Finn' and 'The
Adventures of Tom Sawyer'.

Empire and, not only that, but it had inflicted so great a blow on the empire and its supporters that it had to be made a lesson of for future despots.

Any prospective or potential dictators or autocrats, call them what you may, had to learn the hard way that war carried a heavy penalty and that it was even costlier if, in their grandiose attempt at world rulership, they failed miserably.

The Great War in addition changed how armies got their recruits. For the first time in history, millions upon millions of ordinary civilians, made up of men, women and even teenagers, were either conscripted or volunteered willingly. This meant that a person could be a city-dweller one moment and then very shortly find himself on the front line.

An individual could be a baker, a clerk, a factory worker, a farm hand, or a mechanic - it didn't matter what they had done or were doing, the only condition they had to meet was that they should be willing to die for their country.

If they met this qualification they were welcome into the armed forces with open arms.

You could therefore be a 'butcher, baker, candlestick maker' one minute and then transformed by hard graft into an 'action man' the next; later on, if you survived, you would be called a 'hero' if you did something really, *really* outstanding!

Of course, you couldn't go into the armed forces if you were lame, blind, crippled or decrepit. No, you had to be vigorous or, as it is colloquially said in many parts of the UK, 'full of beans'.

This meant that only the fittest and even those considered down and out, or 'hobos', found that there was now a way open for them to gain respect from the community, to be accepted and to give something instead of waiting for handouts.

Elsie Bartlet,[51] an early recruit to WAAF in 1939, remembers:

'All types turned up to enlist - short, fat, thin, small, dowdy, glamorous, typists and shop girls, married and single, from the all walks of life. They were fussy about who they took at the beginning, and I hadn't a lot going for me - what with spinal curvature and bad eyes.

'However, I slipped in as grade C3 and, by that evening, was in Harrogate with the King's shilling and a sore arm from injections.'

The newspapers were quick to see that even undesirables were being accepted with open arms.

This poem on the following page sent in by Mrs Carling of Milnathort, who was given the scrapbook of Francis Leckie (1919-2007) by her daughters, will bring a fit of laughter from you. (Image below is part of it.)

51 *Forgotten Voices of The Second World War: A new history of world war two in the words of the men and women who were there* by Max Arthur (2005) p17, courtesy Random House Publishing.

George Korankye

The Hobo's Lament

I'm Dusty Dan, of the hobo clan,
And I wander far and near;
But soon, I think, we'll be extinct
For they're calling us up, I hear.

The well-known faces of wide open spaces
Are vanishing now like snow;
I've learned today that they've taken away,
My old pal, Gentleman Joe.

He was always dressed in his granddad's best
(He called my ensemble hideous);
He'll get a commission, or high position,
He was always so fastidious.

Then there's Scribbler Bates, he chalked on gates
To warn us blokes who were nervous;
By his code we found if the house had a hound -
He's gone to the Secret Service.

And hitch-hiking Jock, he never would walk,
We all looked on him as a crank;
He never went far, except in a car -
He's now got a job in a tank.

I'm afraid that the Army would turn me barmy,
My feet couldn't suffer the strain;
And the Navy's no hotter - I never like water
So maybe they'll give me a plane.[52]

---

52 The author traced the origins of Francis Leckie's (1919-2007) scrapbook to *The Sunday Post* (DC Thompson Ltd) who kindly gave permission for its reproduction. Other donations from Francis are in the book with permission being granted.

Those who did not qualify were put into roles that made them feel that they were helping the country.

A HANDY MAN.

Marine (somewhat late for parade). "AT SIX O'CLOCK I WAS A BLOOMIN' 'OUSEMAID; AT SEVEN O'CLOCK I WAS A BLOOMIN' VALET; AT EIGHT O'CLOCK I WAS A BLOOMIN' WAITER; AN' NOW I'M A BLOOMIN' SOLDIER!"

A HANDYMAN

Text: **MARINE (somewhat late for parade: 'At six o'clock I was a bloomin' 'ousemaid: at seven o'clock I was a bloomin' valet; at eight o'clock I was a bloomin' waiter; an' now I'm a bloomin' soldier!'** (©Punch ltd; www.punch.co.uk.)

The first taste that any of these men had of army life was at training camp. To some from 'Civi Street' it was the harshest regime that they had ever experienced. As one recruit said, 'Think of your worst nightmare then multiply it by a thousand'.

To those of us living in the 21st century, the bullyboy tactics used to toughen up these men are difficult to imagine. Yet when you consider what was going on in their lives at that time it is amazing to think that these men and women found room for humour.

Group Captain Frank Care, who served in Burma during 1943, said: 'Humour relieved everybody's feelings'.[53]

They joked about their food, their beds and their unforgiving sergeants. For those in trenches they waxed lyrically about their trench feet, the rats that they slept with and which became their companions. It would be hard not to believe that some of these rats became pets and had their favourite soldier. Did a soldier feel sorry for his ancestors and then decide to bring him home as a souvenir?

Then there was the mud, the glorious mud. Today, women pay good money to have mudpacks plastered on their faces. Well, the mud was free in the trenches. There were no designer clothes in the trenches - everyone eventually looked the same in their latest 'muddy clothes range'.

Caroline Edgley,[54] a Red Cross VAD nurse in a General Hospital in Lincoln, said of the returning soldiers:

'They landed at Lincoln Station and were brought straight up to the hospital with all the clothes that they'd been wearing for the last six weeks or more. You'd have to peel them off them. One man, after he'd been washed and dressed, said he thought he must be in heaven.'

53 *Lest We Forget: Forgotten Voices from 1914-1945* by Max Arthur (2007) p200. Courtesy Random House Publishing.
54 *Women at War* (2002) Courtesy Imperial War Museum Ref: 000515/05.

For a bath to be equated to heaven, it brings home the euphoria the men felt at the thought of a bath. Imagine wearing the same clothes for six weeks or more - no wonder they could still joke about it.

But the mud was nothing compared to the pong. The waft of unwashed men could not be bottled. No amount of expensive perfume could have masked the body odours that filled the trenches. Include to this 'perfume' the acrid whiff of shells, dead and decomposing flesh and you can only try to appreciate what the men had to endure on both sides. The mud and unimaginable whiffs must have been unbearable.

In Caroline's case, mentioned earlier, if the soldier felt that he was in heaven after a good old wash with carbolic soap, what must it have been like for his mates who had to stand beside him? Then again, if everybody whiffed the same no one would notice.

It certainly would be 'the pot calling the kettle black' for any soldier to comment about the odour of another comrade. What it does show is that the conditions the men and women endured were indescribable. No words, prose or poetry could accurately explain what these poor people went through and yet they laughed at their experiences. Isn't it incredible?

Did everyone look forward to a bath? Well, yes and no. William Moore remembers in Tasburgh:

'The army took over Tasburgh Hall as a barracks for a searchlight battalion, a searchlight being on the lawn... various others close by villages...the soldiers were made to wash in the river.

'One soldier hid in the nearby bushes on a severely frosty morning to avoid his wash. He was spotted and thrown in a fairly deep part by NCOs (Non

George Korankye

Commissioned Officers) and left. Little did they know he could not swim!

'My uncle and Mr Ellis were cutting logs nearby and heard some shouting. They both went in the river and rescued the soldier, who was summarily given fourteen days confined to spud peeling.'

Humour is only funny if everyone finds it funny. When you are laughing at someone else's expense then things are not funny.

Usually what happens in such a case is that someone's pride is hurt. In this case a life could have been lost because some fools thought it funny -whether they meant to or not - to drown their kith and kin.

In the above scene, the words of the Talmud would appear to carry some weight: 'Beware of too much laughter, for it deadens the mind and produces oblivion'.

That rule appears to be a good guiding principle to follow in many areas of life, giving birth to the saying 'Everything in moderation'.

Too much of certain things seem not to be good for us, or at times we come across individuals who will carry things too far and thus by their behaviour and speech cause hurt feelings or harm to another human being.

For those who were later to fight in the desert it was the sand that became their test of endurance, the sand and the unbearable and punishable heat. For those in the so-called Arctic convoys it was the cold. In fact, if a person fell into the sea and was not immediately rescued, they could be dead within a few minutes.

The Recruiting Sergeant (on the next page), a scrapbook courtesy of Cliff Grea from Dereham. Notice the soldiers' comments - it seems to be a memorial to himself.

The Recruiting Sergeant

"Swing them arms or I'll tear them off and hit you with the soggy end"!

Cartoon by 'Holly'. Courtesy John Hamlin. [55]

Text: '**Swing them arms or I'll tear them off and hit you with the soggy end!**'[56]

All these stories and images are authentic and help the reader to 'beam back in time', just as the crew of the fictional Star Ship Enterprise were able to do in the famous Star Trek movies and TV programmes.

---

55 Mrs G Gilman of Derby said she was '...having a tidy and sort out...' She sent the above to the author who traced the originator of the image for permission to reprint. This was given together with his life story.

56 Cartoon by 'Holly' Courtesy John Hamlin.

When First I heard the drum of life
Strike up a march so sweetly, O!
I thought I never in my life
Heard music sound so sweetly, O

'By Lance Cpl H Loosemore. Gallipoli twice, Malta
once, France some, Egypt (unclear) and India once.
Wounded 4 June Gallipoli, 1 July France. Brother to
Sergeant A Loosemore VC.'

To get into a humorous mood, a joke by Noel Slevin
of *The Donegal*, a Sunday newspaper, of an Irish recruit
joining the army should bring a smile to anyone's face.
He goes on:

'An Irishman had joined the army and was in the
queue to get his kit. "I don't know my sizes. I'm going to
look a right eejit", he said to the guy in front.

118

"Don't worry," said the other. "You are a little bit bigger than me, so when I say a measurement, you just say the next number."

'The Quartermaster snapped at the guy and the Irishman in turn.

"Boots?"

"Seven," said the guy.

"Eight," said the Irishman.

"Trousers?"

"Thirty-four," said the guy.

"Thirty-five," said the Irishman.

"Shirt collar?"

"Fourteen," said the guy.

"Fifteen," said the Irishman.

"And finally, hat size," the Quartermaster bellowed.

"Six and seven-eighths," said the guy.

"Nine, ten, eleven," said the Irishman.'

This next poem is courtesy of Marion Barbour.[57]

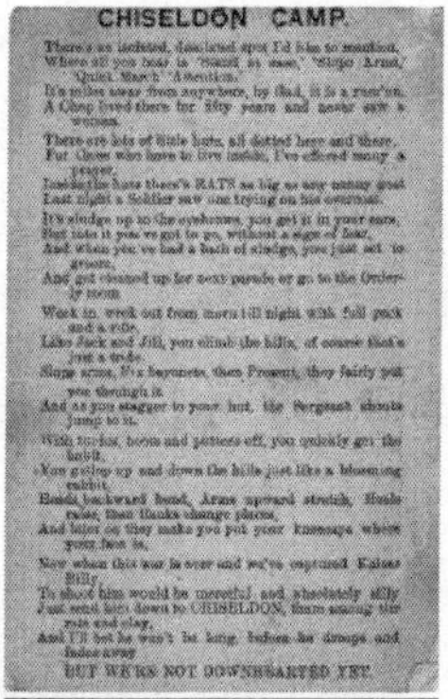
CHISELDON CAMP

BUT WE'RE NOT DOWNHEARTED YET

57 According to Marion, the above poem and other cartoons given to the author '…were sent to my mother from her brothers who were in WW1'.

George Korankye

Chiseldon Camp

There's an isolated, desolated spot I'd like to mention
Where all you hear is 'Stand at ease, Slope Arms
Quick march Attention!'
It's miles away from anywhere by Gad, it is a rum,
um,
A Chap lived there for fifty years and never saw a
woman.
There are lots of little huts all dotted here and there.
For those who have to live inside, I've offered many a
prayer.
Inside the huts there's RATS as big as any nanny goat
Last night a soldier saw one trying on his overcoat.
It's sludge up to the eyebrows, you get it in your ears,
But into it you've got to go, without a sign of fear,
And when you've had a bath of sludge, you just set to
groom,
And get cleaned up for next parade or go to the
Orderly room.
Week in, week out from morn till night with full pack
and a rifle,
Like Jack and Jill, you climb the hills, of course that's
just a trifle
Slope arms, Fix bayonets, then Present, they fairly put
you through it.
And as you stagger to your hut, the Sergeant shouts
'Jump to it'.
With cudgels, boots and puntees off, you quickly get
the habit,
You gallop up and down the hills just like a blooming
rabbit.
Hands backward bend, Arms upward standing, Heads
raised, then Ranks change places,

And later on they make you put your kneecaps where
your face is,
Now when this war is over and we've captured Kaiser
Billy,
To shoot him would be merciful and absolutely silly.
Just send him down to CHISELDON, there among the
rats and clay,
And I'll bet he won't be long, before he droops and
fades away.
BUT WE'RE NOT DOWNHEATRED YET.

Chiseldon Camp eventually housed 12,000 troops.
With so many soldiers coming into such a small
community, problems were bound to occur. One of them
was drink related. William Moore (1934 -)[58] who lived in
Tasburgh remembers his local. He forwarded various
stories to enlighten readers. He recalls:

'...the "Horse Shoes" public house was occupied by
Charles Hales. Early war work saw a change of tenancy
to Sidney Byford, his wife Elsie and one daughter, and
they occupied the pub until their deaths in the 1970s. The
pub never reopened and is now a private house. Sidney
and Elsie Byford were true publicans, friendly,
considerate joining in village activities, organising dart
matches. The football committee meetings were held here
before the village hall was built.
'During the war, beer rationing meant the pub only
opened Friday night, Saturdays, and Sunday night at the

---

58 William Moore sent to the author 'Hard Times and Humour
Tasburgh' (1939-1970). This was a personal reflection of his life. In it
were a few humorous episodes. He would appreciate these being
included. The author is pleased to grant his request. Some of his
stories are featured throughout this book.

most. At the start of the war, soldiers billeted in Tasburgh
Hall would help empty the barrels with the villagers
following. The majority of the soldiers were going
overseas and Americans, arriving at many of the nearby
airbases, soon found local pubs, the Horse Shoe being
one, mostly on cycles, sometimes liberty trucks.

'This usually meant the week's beer was consumed in
one evening, however a barrel would be kept on tap for
the village regulars who enjoyed a daily pint. One would
have to go round the back door and drink it in the cellar.
The local policeman would put his cycle in a field close
by then go back on foot for his refreshments.'

The local bobby getting a free drink? Unheard of.
When did you last hear of a policeman using his authority
to coerce favours? It would never be done now, would it?
Our modern day police are 'straight as a die' are they
not?

In all seriousness, does it not show what is missing
today? The friendliness of the local bobby who knew
everything and who, with a furtive touch of his nose,
would whisper 'nudge, nudge know what I mean?' and
you knew he knew what you were thinking or were about
to do; one who could understand what was happening,
who could put his finger on the pulse of the village.

We have, in the 21st century, progressed in many
ways, but in other ways we have regressed too. In many
parts of the UK there is no longer a community spirit, and
banter with the local bobby is non-existent. He certainly
could not give the vandals a 'clip round the ear' and
march them home to their parents.

They, the parents, would then give the young
'hooligan' ANOTHER clip round the lugholes. If the
local bobby was foolish enough to do so today he would

be out of a job, his pension taken away and perhaps find himself 'on the brew'.

It is now not unheard of for people to live next door to each other and never exchange a greeting. Sad, eh? Truly, you can be in a crowd and paradoxically be alone!

Since drink is being discussed, what is your impression of this poem by William Maylam, conscripted into the army in 1940?

He grabbed me round my slender neck
I could not call or scream
He carried me to his dingy room
Where he could not be seen
He tore away my flimsy wrap
And looked upon my form

I was so cold and damp and scared
Whilst he was hot and warm
His feverish lips he pressed to mine
I gave him every drop
He drained me of my very self
I could not make him stop
He made me what I am today
That's why you find me here
A broken bottle thrown away
That was once full of beer

Ron Goldstein, mentioned in Chapter 1, provides additional valuable information. A story he related proves the above poem by William Maylam is one hundred per cent accurate:

'The campaign in Sicily had been successfully concluded and we were waiting for our next move, the invasion of Italy. Someone at regimental level had decided that the Batteries should put on their own concert parties to entertain the troops and young Lt Whitfield had drawn the short straw. He was now 84 Battery Entertainments Officer.

'In a moment of madness I had volunteered to play a battered "joanna" and other fools had likewise offered to sing, tell jokes or tell monologues, but all this was not enough for Lt Whitfield who obviously considered that this was his moment for show business glory.

"What we are going to do," he proudly told us ("us" being his not over-enthusiastic band of volunteers and pressed men) is to finish the first half of the show with every one on stage singing "Come landlord fill the flowing bowl until it doth run over".

"The clever part," he confidently continued, "is that whilst this is all going on, we will have other chaps coming down the aisles dishing out mugs of vino, which I will organise."

'Came the night, the show went like a dream and we duly sang "Come landlord fill the flowing bowl" as though we meant it.

'Bang on cue, the mugs of vino were brought down the aisles to rapturous applause.

'One slight hitch... the vino was in such quantities that we never got to start the second half of the show, but dear Lt Whitfield has gone down into army folklore history, mine anyway!'

Miss Pocock, from Great Yarmouth, relates that her father (1894-1983) during the outbreak of WW2 was living in Market Drayton and decided to join the army. He joined the Suffolk regiment at Langard Fort and, after basic training, was despatched promptly to 'Bonnie Scotland' where he lived in the shadows of the Forth Rail

Bridge. Who could wish for a more picturesque setting of the rolling hills and glens, tranquil skies and breathtaking scenery. His duties were to protect this strategic bridge, so guess where he found himself? On the island of Inchkeith!

According to Miss Pocock, her father's unit lived in dugouts under the parapets of the rail bridge, on the Leith side of the Forth and they all had to take turns rowing a boat out to Inchkeith, Inchlock and Ince Miccory, to take provisions to the men manning the 'ac-ac' guns on each island. While he was there he wrote a poem:

Marooned

Wail of the Inch-Keith limpits.
Of all the places God has made
Or human feet have strayed
I speak the truth I am not afraid.
It's Inchkeith

It is no place to laze or lurk
Your duties there you cannot skirt
In fact you really have to work,
At Inchkeith.

You cannot see a house for miles,
The cats are prowling on the tiles.
There are neither, hedges, gates, or styles,
At Inchkeith.

There is no church wherein to pray,
And sing, the green hill far away,
All we like sheep have gone astray.
At Inchkeith.

George Korankye

There are no clubs or music halls.
There are no shops or market stalls,
But when it rains the water falls.
At Inchkeith

There are no German sausages here.
No mellow whiskey and no beer.
It makes us feel so very queer.
At Inchkeith

There are no girls to catch the eye.
To give a kiss upon the sly.
For them we have to fume and die.
At Inchkeith

There is a garden for the spud.
There are no roads it's only mud.
It's always wind and rain and flood.
At Inchkeith

Oh could we sling our hooks from here
Enraptured would our hearts appear.
For thee we would not shed a tear
O Inchkeith

With the background knowledge supplied by Miss
Pocock, are you not now in a better position to
understand that poor man's predicament? Here he was
stuck in a miserable pit, miles from home and anyone
who has ever visited Scotland knows that the weather can
be very uninviting.

No social life, miserable weather, miles from home
and he forgot another native of Scotland: the dreaded
midge. This midge is worse than any mosquito; its bite

126

can be likened to that of a snake in that it can drive you absolutely insane, making some scratch themselves so violently that their skin actually starts to bleed.

So famous is the midge that there is actually a song specifically written to it. Yes it is better known than the thistle. The mention of the midge strikes fear and terror into the hearts of all residents in Scotland.

Not only songs have been written about it, but products have been designed and creams have been concocted from all kinds of ingredients, but still this hardy little creature has outwitted them all. It is Scotland's secret weapon against any invader.

It is reputed to have kept the Romans out - that is why they built the two walls, Antoine and Hadrian, to make sure that the dreaded midge stayed where it was.

Had the Germans been foolish enough to try to invade Britain there is no doubt about it: they would have been stopped by this ruthless army of assassins who come out by day and strike their foe, leaving then absolutely demented.

The Midge Song

By Alistair Reid[59]

I was born and bred in Scotland, and I'm very proud to be,
A native of this country, where the air is clean and free.
It's fine to be in Scotland, but the itch is gettin' worse
For out among the countryside, I met wi' Scotland's curse.

---

59 www.incallander.co.uk/scottishsongs.htm

It hides among the bushes, and it lurks among the grass,
Beside the Loch and up the hill, it waits for you to pass.
The one that's first to find you, soon will tell three million more.
And suddenly the swarm descends, each one a carnivore.

Quite soon they're getting in your hair, and always up your nose,
And in your ears and in your eyes, and underneath your clothes.
They'll suck your blood and soon those itchy spots will start to swell.
The spots join up when you're in bed, you'll think you've gone to hell.

So you'll go and ask the chemist for the latest kind of spray.
That's tried and tested, even proved, to keep the pest away.
And plastered ower wi' midgey cream, that smells so very bad,
You'll flap your arms and run around, and act as if you're mad.

You'll button up your clothes, and buy the famous midgey hood,
It's guaranteed to stop you, from becoming midgey food.
But save yourself the trouble, for the time will come to pass,

When a midge will crawl right up your leg, and bite
you on the Knee.

The tourists often wonder why, the kilt is seldom
seen,
And Scottish accent never heard, in places they have
been.
For at winter's end, the Scots all go to Tenerife, or
Spain.
And they leave behind the midges, and the cold, and
wind, and rain.

Now I think I've found the cure at last, my itching
now has ceased.
No longer am I willing, to provide a midgey feast.
For I changed my job and moved away, to London
I've gone down.
Cos I reckon even midges couldn't live in London
Town

Chorus
I had bites on my fingers and bites on my thumb,
Bites on my belly and bites on my bum.

And somewhere else - and somewhere else - and
somewhere else.

However, the various training camps during various
wars of the last century all had firing ranges. This was an
opportunity for some soldiers to vent their feelings about
'subalterns' (an officer in the British Army) in a
humorous way because of the way that they were being
treated. In both wars, training camps thus became a
hotbed for humour.

George Korankye

Text: **'Little more to the right and on your target.'**[60]

Wendy Kingshott, who sent the above cartoon, said the production of the rag *Petroc News* '...was very labour intensive with hand typed articles and pen and ink cartoons...I have picked out the best of the cartoons...I think it is wonderful that although things were so fraught then, and with their obviously *limited resources they still found space for some humour'* (italics author's).

We must not also forget the enforcement of rank in society at that time too. There was a clear demarcation among the classes. So when a person joined the army these demarcations were strictly adhered to.[61]

---

60 Wendy Kingshott from East Sussex donated an assortment of cartoons and stories from her father, Frederick Powell, who, according to her '...was in the Royal Army Pay Corp stationed in Devon during WW2. He was editor of a magazine called *The Petroc Paragon News* produced in 1943...'

61 Donated by Wendy Kingshott from East Sussex.

Again, the men found time to poke fun at their superiors. Although the aspect of individuality and equality were emphasised, this was not always the case and once again fun was made of this philosophy

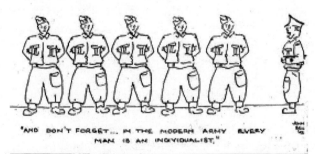

Text: **'And don't forget in the modern army everyone is an individualists,' says Sergeant Major.**[62]

---

62 Donated by Wendy Kingshott from East Sussex.

George Korankye

Text: **Officer: 'Why(!) didn't you salute me?'**
PTE Chappie: 'I gave you eyes right, Sir; as I was
carrying 4 eggs in one hand and 3 in the other.'[63]
Officer: 'Where are the eggs?!!'

What about the demon drink? Drink was to blame for so many vices that it led to the prohibition in America in the 1920s.

With all the negative press that drink gets you may wonder if any good can ever come from it. Well, you will be surprised to find out that, yes, the good old 'demon drink' has its uses. Consider this story from Heather Crooks who lives in Preston:

'My grandfather, Edwin Preston, was in the Lancashire Fusiliers. To enable him to send more money home during the First World War he worked in the mess and became known to many of the officers. Whilst fighting in the then Mesopotamia he was wounded. He was on a log trying to get across a river, whilst being shot at. He did get shot in the leg and managed to get to the riverbank where he spent two days in the bushes.

---

63 Donated by Wendy Kingshott from East Sussex.

'Luckily the Red Cross found him while searching for the wounded. He said at the time he wished he would die, for the pain was unbearable. The bullet went in the front and out of the back. His leg was shattered. They took him along an unmade road in a cart drawn by oxen, a hell of a journey to a hospital.

'The poison from the wound made him delirious for months. When he was recovering he was sat in a chair on a pavilion, when one of the officers he used to serve in the mess was doing the rounds. He looked at him and said, "Good God, is that you Preston? How on earth have you got in this bloody mess?"

'He gave him a flask of brandy which my grandfather swore saved his life. He would take a daily swig of it and pour a little on his wound. He always said he wouldn't have made it without it. He was eventually taken to India and had to wait two years for a boat home. The one that he was meant to be on was too overloaded to take him. Unfortunately it got blown up not long after it had left the harbour. He was lucky to be put on another a few days later, and sailed safely home. His injury stayed with him all his life, though he worked hard as a builder well into his seventies.'

There is an old saying that goes, 'You will drink yourself into an early grave'. Well, that is not precisely correct in this case. It could be argued that drink saved Edwin Preston from an early grave!

Another notable Officer joke was by William Maylam conscripted into the army in 1940:

Officer: 'Didn't you see me coming up the lines?'
Recruit: 'Yes Sir'
Officer: 'Then why didn't you ask who goes there?'

133

Recruit: 'Why, hang it, Sir, I've known you since you were a kid.'

Another of Hallam's jokes: 'How do they open the locks of the Panama Canal? By using the quays of course, you ignorant blighter!'

George McMillan from Perth recollects the shenanigans about a particular parcel. His Uncle John, who was serving in the North African desert in World War Two, received a letter at Christmas from his wife, Agnes, who was droll, if not eccentric. It read:

'The Church Women's Guild handed in a parcel for you for Christmas and asked me to send it on. There was a packet of 50 cigarettes but, as you don't smoke, I gave them to the postman. There were also a pair of gloves, a scarf and a warm pullover but, as you're in the desert, you won't be needing them in all that heat and I gave them to the next-door neighbour.

'The ladies included a box of chocolates, but they were plain chocolate and I know you don't like them, so I ate them myself. They were very good.

'Finally, I found stationery, but you won't need that as all your mail is sent by aerograph, which has to be reduced and needs special paper. I kept the stationery. There was nothing left to send you, but don't forget to write and thank the Women's Guild for the parcel!

'Your ever-loving wife, Agnes.

'PS Wasn't that kind of the ladies of the Women's Guild - very thoughtful!'

John did get some benefit from the letter and non-existent parcel.

He read the letter out to his mates and they fell about laughing - a real tonic for the Desert Rats.

He kept the letter and must have read it out a thousand times to other soldiers throughout the war before finally bringing it home as a souvenir.

Agnes never did understand why people laughed at her letter. That was a true story!'

It was not just the officers that came in for some ribbing, as Peter Steggall recounts:

'At the training camp in Surrey, we had to march and rifle drill under a ferocious sergeant, whose commands were shouted so vehemently that his false teeth were sometimes expelled from his mouth, but he became very adept at catching them in mid-air!!

'Our laughter was inevitably the cause of another outburst of foul expletives.'

64

---

[64] Cartoon by Jordon Krawczyk

What he remembers was a 'wido' who was 'trying to work his ticket'- slang for trying to get discharged -who just could not get things right. He just could not learn anything, in fact he could not keep either himself, his kit and quarters clean, was absolutely frustrating - so frustrating that his drilling was a waste of time.

Peter goes on to relate:

'He seemed to be unable to learn anything or to keep himself and his quarters clean and tidy. When reprimanded for singing on parade one day he replied "there aint no law against singing, sarge!"'

Well, readers, with the characteristics of the sergeant depicted above, perhaps you can supply your own ending to the reaction of the sergeant. It is highly unlikely that the sergeant would have said 'carry on singing, son. I am sure we will all be encouraged by your fine dulcet tones'.

Another incident that Peter remembers is that of a big burly chap standing in a queue waiting for his inoculation. But guess what happened? Why, the poor 'chappie' fainted! And guess where he landed? Into a large puddle of water.

You can imagine the scene: a big burly chap lying in a puddle with all the other soldiers killing themselves laughing. My! If that chappie was a bully, surely this was an incident that could be used to help him to have empathy for his fellow soldiers.

Interestingly, Peter says he was in the army by default or by chance. He had initially wanted to join the Royal Navy but, 'when registering on 1 April 1941…after a medical examination I was dismissed very brusquely by a naval officer with the words "You're no good to us, boy! You're….blind".'

One incident happened during the last phases of the war in Germany in 1945. Peter enumerates:

'A kit inspection by the Orderly Officer and the Regimental Sergeant-Major was enlivened by a young soldier who had not laid out his kit as prescribed. On being reprimanded he picked up his kit-bag, opened the top, and swung it round and round scattering the contents all over the room.'

Well, the officers did not know how to react. Everybody was stunned, but the whole mess burst out laughing. Whether it was because of his sheer stupidity, a nervous reaction, or the bravery of doing such an unthinkable thing in front of everyone, it beggars belief what Peter's old training sergeant would have said to that young soldier in Germany. Would his teeth have come flying out? If so, would he have been able to find them among all the contents of the kit bag? You, the reader, can supply your own ending!!!

Of course, we cannot forget the role of women in the armed forces, but were they welcomed with open arms? Let us hear from someone who was there. Elizabeth Lee's story is a tribute to women's fortitude and a refusal to give into a stereotypical image.

To get some background knowledge, she had a brother who owned a garage. So, unlike females of her generation, she had acquired technical skills in vehicle maintenance and repair. This knowledge was to become her lifesaver. It was going to be a bulwark against the macho image that prevailed. Anyway, because she was a woman when she volunteered her services and was assigned to Army Service Corps, she was put on a month's trial to see how she would fair.

The question on the minds of all the top brasses was, could these women hack it? Were they cut out for such a role or given a bit of pressure would they pack up like a deck of cards? What had escaped these people's notice was that the women had proved their metal in a lot of ways.

Did not most of these women lump coal into the house every day to keep the fires burning? Did they not keep the houses spick and span? Did they not prepare meals every day and take care of the children?

On top of that, did not some also do other jobs to make ends meet?

Now, in the early 20th century, there was no such thing as a big supermarket with all things under one roof, no vacuum cleaners or all the convenient household equipment that we have today. In fact, even clothes were usually repaired at home.

There is no doubt about it, a woman's lot was indeed hard, yet many men at that time felt that these workers were weaklings and should stay in the kitchens.

So obviously, with this kind of prevailing view, it is no wonder that they were not welcome with open arms into the armed forces. Those that tried to prove the men wrong found themselves in hot water.

Over to Elizabeth Lee[65] who volunteered in the First World War:

'We were each given one of these thirty hundredweight vans and the men led us a devil of a life. They'd cut a petrol pipe half-through, they'd unscrew a valve and they'd change over the leads on the sparking plugs. They'd empty oil out of your lamps (because they

---

65 *Women At War* (2002). Courtesy Imperial War Museum Ref: 000779/16.

was all paraffin lamps). The girls dropped out one by one.

'We had to do a lot of driving and they would give us the wrong directions. Some of us knew our way around the area but many of us didn't. The sergeant backed the men up. He always gave us the dirtiest jobs to do - if it was a coal heaving job we had to do it, or if it was to find an out of the way place, it fell on the girls.

'The men resented women in the army. Every time a woman went in the army, they were transferred elsewhere, out to France, overseas.

'At the end of the month there was just two of us left. But they couldn't get much wrong with me, because I knew more that a good many of them did. And also I was cunning enough to always be prepared with a bit of stiff binding tape in case there was a leak in my petrol, and I looked at my tyres and tested them...

'When we had a tool inspection they'd pinch our tools, so that we were short of tools. You know, all sorts of nasty little niggly things that they'd do because they didn't want us. They wanted to try us out, because on the whole they were nice chaps. There were a couple of beastly ones, but to them it was a lark, for kicks.

'Anyway, when we passed our test there were two of us that were taken on. They couldn't have been nicer to us, we were one of them then. One of them said to me one day, "Sorry we led you such a dance, but we didn't want women drivers". They wanted fun in other ways but it didn't work out. It did with some of them, but not with me.'

Was she alone? No, another example is that of Ruby Ord:[66]

---

66 *Women At War* (2002). Courtesy Imperial War Museum Ref: 44/5.

'We were training for two weeks. It was awful. We were at Hastings, which was very nice, but we had to get up about six and do PT and go for a march. We were drilled in the square and were the laughing stock of all the men, which was absurd, because none of us had ever done this sort of drill that the army does – form fours and all sorts of section drill. So some people's right was my left and vice-versa.

'We then went for a route march before breakfast, and our last meal had probably been before seven the night before, and not adequate anyway – not for people straight from home, where mother took jolly good care that you had plenty, and a glass of milk before you went to bed.

'We came back to a terrible breakfast: semi-raw herring and that sort of thing, you just couldn't eat it. So the little bit of money we had we spent as soon as we could get free from the fetter, and dashed to the nearest café.

'We were also inoculated twice, and vaccinated – inoculated and vaccinated in one morning, so that quite a lot of the girls went down like ninepins. We were pretty miserable. We were washing in tin basins in a room with a row of basins – well, we weren't accustomed to washing in company. So we were adjusting very slowly. We had some very nice NCOs there, the Women's Voluntary Reserve. They were the suffragettes. But they had no control.

'Making troops of us I always resented. I didn't join an army, I always want to be a woman. I don't want the status of women to be established as women: I don't want to be given equality with men because I feel we are a bit superior. So that has always shocked me. I thought men used to look up to women. You don't look up to your equal.'

The funny thing is, because of the way some men had treated women in the past, did you notice the tone of Ruby Ord? She was not striving for equality, but superiority. Sadly, her view came to epitomise those of some women.

Mrs Stuart, who became a VAD nurse in 1939, writes:

'My husband was posted to command the Jungle Warfare School at Dusan Tua near Kuala Lumpur.

'By 1 April 1946 I had managed to get permission to join him from Calcutta. We had two EP IP leaky tents joined together over which our Japanese prisoners of war, who were awaiting repatriation, built a roof.

'They also gave me a huge tray on which they had built a model of a Japanese village using cigarette packets and their silver paper and anything else they could find. I was very sorry indeed not to be able to take it to India when we left for our next posting.

'When John went out on Night Exercises, he always left me a pistol, "just in case".

'One night, when he was out, I heard stealthy sounds coming from the front entrance. I raised the pistol and then heard a familiar voice: "Don't shoot. I forgot the maps!"'

Ron Goldstein relates another story:

'Alf Goddard of Birmingham was an impatient type of man, always on the go and barely avoiding trouble, as he had an infectious grin permanently all over his face. One day, during the winter stalemate of 1944 in the North of Italy, the tanks were all bogged down and so the powers that be decided that the whole brigade should stand on the winter line along the Senio River as infantry.

'On the south side of the river, therefore, we were in houses lining the riverbank, and the German infantry were also in houses along the north side of the river. Nothing was happening and boredom soon became paramount. This was not Goddard's style and so he made his way up to the attic, opened the window, leaned out, aimed his rifle, and fired a shot - which brought down the opposing house's chimney pot which rolled down and dropped on the front door step. Whereupon the front door opened, a German came out, inspected the broken chimney pot, slammed the door and could be heard running up the stairs to his attic.

'He also leaned out the window and brought down Goddard's chimney pot. This looked like good fun and pretty soon all of the houses were minus their chimney pots. A few days later the army newspaper declared with banner headlines that "heavy fighting had broken out at the Senio".'[67]

Not much has changed really. How many times has something been reported in the media which has been blown out of proportion, or perhaps we have made assumptions about individuals and people, etc, only to find on reflection our views were mistaken. It is very likely you will recollect an incident. Is it not wise in any situation to carefully consider the Greek proverb, 'Don't hear one and judge two before jumping to conclusions'? The scenario concerning the search for weapons for mass destruction in Iraq is an example that springs to mind.

Wars, it has been shown, affect all and sundry. However more than anything else the war changed the attitudes of a nation about a particular group. Who were

67 Ron Goldstein, WW2 People's War. Courtesy BBC.

this group? The following chapter discusses this group and the humour that resulted because of changing attitudes.

Ending this chapter on a light note, World War Two was also a 'popular war' in that the country saw it as a fight against good and evil. Even the 'glorious dead' could get involved. Robert the Bruce (1274-1329), and King of Scotland (1274-1329), a dead Scottish Freedom Fighter could even be recruited to help the 'Desert Rats'.

From *The Petroc News* another resurrected image:

Text: **'Back later gone to El Alamein, BRUCE.'**

Text: As you are supposed to be resting in a quiet spot, a litt'e light literature goes well.

Text: In every section there is at least one musical genius to cheer you up when you feel downhearted. Generally he plays a penny whistle.

Text: A regular carouse of coffee and fried eggs is one of the things we always have when we get to one of these villages.

Text: A comfortable bed at last!

Text: Sometimes when you are out on rest you think you'd almost rather stop in the trenches.

Both sides shown to confirm date and censor authenticity.

Text: It looks rather pretty to see a picture of us at dinner in the yard of one of our billets doesn't it?

Text: Ain't it nice to get into a town once more!

Top right: Russian White Army recruitment poster, 1919.
"Why aren't you in the army?"

Left: Yiddish-language recruitment poster for the Jewish
Legion published in American Jewish magazines during World
War I. Daughter of Zion (representing the Jewish people): רעייא
.טענמיגער ןעשידיא םעד ןיא ןָא ךיז טסילש !ןעבאָה ךייד ץראַד דנאַלייַנטלאַ
"Your Old New Land must have you! Join the Jewish
regiment.") Right: Paulista Constitutionalist propaganda poster,
1932. "You have a duty to follow. Check your conscience."

Waffen-SS propaganda poster, 1944. "You Too! Your comrades await in the French Division of the Waffen-SS."

United States, 1917. J M Flagg's Uncle Sam recruited soldiers for World War I and World War II.

Chapter 6

The Role of Women

'Laughter is the sun that drives winter from the
human face'
Victor Hugo (1802 – 1885)

It cannot be overemphasised the effect that the Great War
had on women. It speeded up a process of
'emancipation', freedom, liberation and a 'coming out of
the kitchens' in droves. A trendy tune in the 1970s by the
female group Sister Sledge was: 'We are Family' (1979)
with the rhyming chorus *sisters are doing it for
themselves*. This ballad was to be taken up by the
liberated women of the 1960s and 1970s to signify that
women could now literally do things for themselves. To
fully understand what was happening, you have to look at
the period just before 1914.

At that time women were employed mostly in the
domestic sector. Oh, there were one or two who held
responsible posts, but let's not make any bones about it:
these were indeed few and far between! Men were like a
bulldog trying to cling onto its bone, tenaciously resisting
women's advancements into any profession that they
considered to be 'their's'.

Men would not give up this 'bone' of autocracy,
tyranny and dictatorship without a fight! Are these words
too harsh? It was not a case of 'my country right or
wrong'. No! According to the men of the pre-war

generation, as far as they were concerned it was 'my profession, no women, right or wrong'.

The female gender was classified as weak. They were temptresses, not as intelligent as men, in fact we could go on and on about the physical, emotional and psychological abuses that women suffered. The attitudes that most men held about women would be considered derogatory, defamatory, offensive and, in layman's terms, 'downright wrong', in fact illegal in many countries of the 21st century.

Obviously not all men held such views of women, but it can honestly be said that the vast majority of men held to the old saying 'a woman's place is in the home', a proverb similar to the view that was held about children: 'children should be seen and not heard'. Yes, according to this popular view a child's opinion was considered 'forward' or precocious and they 'should only speak when spoken to'. To be frank, even in the 21st century there are still countries on this planet that still cling doggedly to this antiquated view of women and children.[68]

What came to the women's rescue? Was it the Suffragettes, or perhaps the enlightened sympathisers of women of the day - the Liberals, as they came to be known? Maybe the mass grumblings or nagging of women of their men-folk at home evoked a mass shift in attitude towards them?

It would be fair to say all these things played a role. However, without question, the Great War provided a

---

68 It is not the remit of this book to discuss the role of women or their advancement in the 20th and into the 21st century. Certainly women have come a long way, but for a more enlightening view the reader can turn to *The Women's Century* by Mary Turner (2004) and *Women at War* by Nigel Fountain (2007).

catalyst, a vehicle that the mass movements of women's emancipations could now ride.

Women were now on a crest of a wave. Even those women's movements that had been vocal in their condemnation of possible conflicts threw their hat into the ring or, to be precise, threw the towel in. They abandoned en-masse their opposition movement, a few going as far as renouncing their hunger strikes and violent campaigns. Why the sudden change in tactics?

The simple reason was due to the fact that a large number of men had been called to war leaving a huge gap in the labour market. To get an idea of the labour shortages, consider the fatalities in just one battle alone during the Great War, in which over 57,000 men were victims. This was in one day!

A new situation had thus inadvertently been created, a situation unique to mankind, a state of affairs never before encountered. Women were now in uncharted waters. The questions were, firstly, how did the women react, secondly, how would they steer this 'oil tanker' they were in and, thirdly, how did the men - the politicians, those still in employment 'keeping the camp fires burning' at home - react?

Yes, how would the men on the 'ship' who now found themselves with new or additional 'crew mates' respond? Would they look upon women as challenging the male macho image or would they accept them with open arms? It would have been surprising if they had been welcoming, shaking their hands, hugging them and receiving them warmly into the workplace.

Look at any organisation, any place of work trying to bring in new procedures, new methods of working and what happens? Look back to any mighty union struggle in the 20th century between workers and bosses and what was the one bone of contention? Yes, change to working practices. If you don't have 'a union ticket' you can't do this job, was a well known phrase. Introduction of new machines that replaced humans has always caused troubles; a case in point is the luddites.[69]

There will be, and there always has been, the inevitable resistance to change. Yes, as the traditionalists say, 'a new broom sweeps clean'.

No change comes about without resistance. It was inevitable, predictable, 'as clear as mud' that men would cling to their positions. The old grumblings will be heard over and over again: If it's not broke why fix it? Another aspect of change is not just in attitude; it also has to do with the way lots of us are. Some of us are selfish and tend to think more of ourselves than others. To exemplify this point, consider the experience of Private Dolly Shepherd of Women's Emergency Corps.[70] After her initial training in 1914 she goes on:

'One day we had a route march to Mansion House (in London), and of course people were giggling and laughing and saying: "Women soldiers! Just imagine having women soldiers. Whoever thought of such a thing!" They certainly sneered at us.'

---

69 The Luddites were more of a social movement than a political one. They were not like the suffragettes who were later to campaign for voting rights for women. They were more like the skilled labour force of the 20th century and were employed in the textile industries in the early part of the 19th century. Their industrial action consisted of destroying their mechanised weaving looms because of changes to working practices that the Industrial Revolution (late 18th and early 19th century) was bringing about.

70 *Forgotten Voices of The Great War: A new history of world war two in the words of the men and women who were there* by Max Arthur (2003) p25. Courtesy Random House Publishing.

Statistics also sheds an important light on the changes in women's fortunes before and after the Great War.[71]

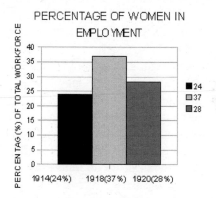

Interestingly, Professor Bourke calculates that approximately 12 per cent of the female population in England and Wales were in domestic service in 1911 and yet by 1931 this had fallen to 8 per cent.[72]

Where had all the domestic servants gone? They had gone to work in the factories, others the expanding civil services, others even into heavy industries. Professor Bourke estimates that Civil Service numbers increased from 33,000 in 1911 to 102,000 by 1921, while a staggering 50 per cent of new drivers in London Transport were women.

---

[71] In 1914 it was estimated 24 per cent of the total British Workforce were women by 1918 it increased to 37 and fell to 28 per cent as men took up employment once again after WW1. Source see footnote 72.

[72] Professor Joanna Bourke: *Women on the Home front in World War*
www.bbc.co.uk/history/british/britain_wwone/women_employment_0 1.shtml

With so many women in the workplace, this proved a productive ground for humour. How would men accept them? Would their sexuality be taken advantage of? What exactly were the prevailing attitudes? Certainly, men resisted the advancement of women, especially in the area of voting.

A number of employers took advantage of the situation by embracing this new labour pool, but not at the same wages that they paid men. They paid them a fraction of the cost, thus coercing a few female employees to reluctantly accept a reduced wage structure since there were no alternative means of work.

Their men-folk were off to do their duty for 'king and country', a number destined never to return. Cases came to light where a number of females now found themselves as the sole breadwinner, resulting in what became known as 'role reversal'.

A possible scenario could be a wounded returnee with no pension or income support, no child benefit or Statutory Sick Pay, and only relying on either charity or handouts. They still had to be supported, resulting in a woman finding herself in the unenviable position of providing for her brood, a fact a considerable portion of men could not accept and felt it was dereliction of their duties

Bear in mind that the National Insurance in its current form with all its benefit payments came about initially in 1911 by an Act of Parliament: the National Insurance Act 1911. It was further improved in 1946 by Clement Atlee. Payments to 'deserving cases' were therefore in its infancy during the war years. Improvements only resulted as a direct consequence of feedback from the public and various bodies, highlighting difficulties and cases the Act was neglecting.

This tide of unstoppable women clamouring for votes or suffrage became a 'cause celebre'. It was a controversial issue, a banner for all women to get under to achieve a momentum that proved relentless in challenging what was perceived as man's god given domain.

The battle for women's suffrage once again can be traced to the Great War, which many claim was the catalyst for their triumph in achieving the vote. But even before the Great War, women's attitudes were changing.

Text: **Primum Vivere, Deine Philosophari (first one must live, then one may philosophise). 'Is Florrie's engagement really off, then?' 'Oh, yes. Jack wanted her to give up gambling and smoking, and goodness knows what else.' (Chorus) 'How absurd!!'**[73]

The cartoon above by *Punch* would have brought hilarious laughter in the smoke-filled, gin-swigging rooms of the common bars and alehouses and even illicit drinking dens! Picture some gin-swilling man saying: 'Do you know, they will be wanting the vote next and

---

73 *Punch*, 25 January 1905.

before you know it we will be having a female prime minister. Ridiculous I say, Oi, chaps! Ha! Hah! Ha!'

How Margaret Thatcher, Prime Minister of the UK (1979-1990), must be laughing. Is she not reputed to have said: 'If you want anything said, ask a man. If you want something done, ask a woman'?

Moving closer toward 1914, the attitudes and perceptions of women begin to change. A catalyst that enabled this transformation or metamorphosis, this inactive weak pupa to develop into a butterfly able to support itself must surely have been the way that the suffragettes were willing to resort to violence to achieve their aims. This new breed of 'ninja women' was a direct backlash because of the progressive mal-treatment of women over the centuries.

THE SUFFRAGETTE THAT KNEW JIU-JITSU.
The Arrest.

The cartoon below by *Punch* shows that not all men considered 'women a weaker vessel'.

Text: **The Suffragette that Knew Jiu-Jitsu. The Arrest.**[74]

Is this a caricatured case of 'beware the woman scorned'? In fact, the actual quote wrongly attributed to Shakespeare was composed by William Congreve (1670-

74 Punch, 6 July 1910.

1729) for his play 'The Mourning Bride' (1697). The genuine verses are 'Heaven has no rage like love to hatred turned. Nor hell a fury like a woman scorned.'

A secret weapon that could have brought countless women to their knees is spiders. Had the government of the day used the dreaded spider it could have stopped the suffragettes in their tracks. When they started marching in their droves, all the policemen had to do was line the streets and release hundreds and millions of spiders.

Is this far fetched? Not actually. Newly declassified documents released into the public domain shows how a member of the public wrote to Scotland Yard during WW2 of a grave concern that he had. It was a matter of national security as far as he was concerned. It appears that the he thought the IRA would resort to subterfuge to undermine the British will. He felt that having failed to destabilise the public by its bombing campaigns it would then go to London Zoo and release all the spiders, creating mass hysteria and thus a kind of national arachnophobia would ensure.[75]

This, one supposes, would tie up all the psychiatrists. Chemists would be inundated with requests for calming medication. Before the invention of tranquillisers, this would pose a slight problem. Finding their herbal medication ineffective, the women would then turn to the illicit drug dealers' pedalling their opiate drugs.

This person then goes on to mention that, as spiders do not breed like rabbits but breed as spiders, it would not be long before the country is overrun by these eight-legged creatures, resulting in valuable police time and resources being used to eliminate spiders. Now, whether this person's assertions and fears were taken seriously or

---

75 Courtesy National Archives MEPO3/1143.

not, the documents do not mention. The fact is here was a secret weapon that the government during WW1 failed to utilise when it was trying to keep the suffragette movements in check. Imagine the fear and panic among the suffragettes as they debated about the infiltrators in their midsts, these eight-legged traitors whose main aim was to destroy this embryonic organisation.

But did all women welcome with open arms this new awakening of their consciences? No! The cartoon below shows that resistance came from within their own gender who saw this as women rising above their station, trying to be something that were not created for or had the capacity to successfully manage.

Text: **Spread of the servant girl graduate idea** *(Interior of a super-kitchen.)* *Mistress.* **'Would you mind leaving your Sophocles for a moment, Mary, and run to the shop?'**[76]

---

76 *Punch*, 8 December 1913, courtesy Gutenberg project.

The suffragettes campaigned, in fact preached with religious zeal, the thought that giving women equal rights would liberate them, that it would help them free their shackles of slavery and open up a world that hitherto they could only peer over the parapet at.

The changing roles of women was a burning issue; a great cause of division was in the making. Did the Great War rescue not just women but the whole nation from a violent confrontation? Some say 'yeh' others 'nay'.[77]

The Great War thrust women in a role that could not be reversed once the war was over. The genie had been let out of the bottle and it was not willing to go back into captivity.

In a way there were very few options open to men if they had not grasped the nettle. Why? With so many deaths they had to find replacements.

Widescale immigration from the colonies was not an option, as Britain had thrown some of the cream of its colonies into action, and neither was conscription or volunteering. These had all been carried out.

The only avenue open to the government was an untapped workforce who would replace the depleting males - women. There is no doubt about it that the war brought about a dramatic change for women. In fact, one genuine story that would be hard to believe when you consider all the above negative attitudes that prevailed about women during the First World War is that of Helen Pease.[78] What do you think of this incident that happened to her:

---

77 For a more detailed discussion of whether the Great War contributed to women's suffrage, see *The Women's Century: A Celebration of Changing Roles 1900-2000* by M Turner p47.

78 *Women At War* (2002) Courtesy Imperial War Museum Ref 821/20.

'At Hayes Munitions Factory they'd got five thousand girls. Most of these girls have never been in a factory before. They'd probably done home sewing, the sort of things they did, London girls, when they wanted to earn their livings. The management was all men.

'One day the telephone call came through to the office in Bloomsbury. For God's sake, send some of your organisers down here. The girls are all hysterical. And they've chased me into the office. The manager, if you please. I've locked myself in. Madeline Simons and I were off down there. We found five thousand girls, raging hysteria, shrieking, yelling and throwing the furniture about.

'Madeline Simons stood up, a very beautiful woman with a Parisian dress on, and talked to them in a quiet way. Finally we got them to choose some of their number to make a committee to join the union to come and talk to the management.

'The row had officially arisen when somebody had found a cigarette end in the rice pudding. Madeline and I got a group of about eight girls to go along and see the manager. He said to us: "I'm quite used to dealing with men. I've never had to deal with women before. For heaven's sake go up and keep them quiet". It was really very funny, especially when you think we were both of us twenty-two and twenty-one and had no experience.

'They produced some sort of settlement they were able to discuss and some of the girls joined the union. And, you know, there was then some organisation which could talk to the management. There were no shop stewards, of course, no unions at all. And the men's unions wouldn't touch the women at that time. They didn't want women's unions and women to take men's work.'

The author gave Jordon the brief of illustrating the factory scene. He was told to envision the time line of the book - from pre-1914 to the current time - and try to incorporate all the characters into his illustration. Has he succeeded?[79]

Visualise that poor bloke, absolutely terrified of 5,000 screaming women. Is it every man's worst nightmare, or would some men love to have the attention of thousands of screaming women?

Now if this happened today, can you imagine the tabloids getting a hold of the story? Some headlines would be downright rude. Others would be 'risqué'. Then there would be the analysts, the physcologists offering all their different interpretations and the cartoons, my they would have a field day.

Now fast forward yourself from WW1 to WW2 and what awaits the onlooker? My, oh my, a totally different scene - women actually working in a shipyard! Could there be a more male-dominated place of work?

For the sake of simplicity, picture pre WW2 before women arrived onto the shipyard. A burly ship-worker drops a hammer on his toe. Can you think of the expletives and the colourful language that would follow such an action? But once women came into the picture there appears to be a change in language and attitude.

---

79 Cartoon by Jordon Krawczyk.

George Korankye

You can now imagine a burly ship-worker after dropping a hammer on his toe saying, 'Oh dear, I've just dropped a hammer on my toe. What a silly Billy I am!'

This kind of 'mickey taking' was evidence of the humour that greeted women. Some fully supported the role of women. They felt that it made the work place more jovial and balanced. Others were not so accommodating.

The Shipyard Poem

We used to be called the toughest of men,
Fearing neither the devil, the sword, nor the pen;
But those days are departed, sadly, amen!
Since the women came into the shipyard.

We used to rip open the day with an oath,
'Get tore inta a gaffer' we never were loathe,
Now a gentle 'good-morn' is how we greet both
Since the women came into the shipyard.

'Gie's ower that!! Hammer, ye big!! Lump o' cheese'
'Get oot o' ma !! road, or I'll melt ye in grease',
Now we make each request with a sweet 'if you please'
Since the women came into the shipyard.

'Tis wondrous the change that's come over this place,
The studious attention man pays to his face,
His manners, his habits, his undreamed of grace -
Since the women came into the shipyard.

And when that time comes - it's not too far away -
All earth a fair heaven, less work and more play,
Historians will tell it began on that day -
Since the women came into the shipyard.

Talking of shipyards, a well-known shipbuilding community was the Clyde, based in Scotland. Mention of the Clyde conjures up Glaswegians. Since women are being discussed, perhaps you will enjoy this tale by L King, who lives in Cumbernauld:[80]

'My family was friendly with a Polish soldier who lived in the home of a lady in the village to where we were evacuated during the war. Every morning his landlady would shout "Yup yit?" at breakfast time and for months he hadn't a clue what she was saying. Eventually my mum explained she was saying, "Are you up yet?"'

We know thousands of Polish soldiers were billeted in Scotland and the mind boggles at the thought of the 'natives' trying to teach them English. You can just imagine some Scottish school child going to his mum saying:

'I can speak Polish, Ma.'

'Aye that'll be right,' says the wee yin's mum. 'What Polish word have yee learned then?'

---

80 Courtesy *Sunday Post*, 8 June 2008.

'Cheery Blossom, Ma,' says the cheeky blighter.

For those of a certain age you will remember Cherry Blossom is the trademark for a well-known brand of 'shoe polish'.

Women became indispensable in the workplace. One author says that without their contribution the war may have gone a different way. Women volunteered in their millions. Some even joined the armed forces, as in the case of Mrs Stuart, who wrote:

'In January 1939, I became a VAD nurse. I was on Night Duty on a Ward of some thirty eye patients evacuated from London because of the Blitz. Soon after midnight, I heard a plane pass over-head and then an enormous bang. I grabbed a torch and ran round the Ward but no one moved!

'One man was an awful nuisance and soon to go home. He would not wake up in the morning when we were trying to get our work done before the Day Staff arrived at 8am.

'He complained about the food, his bed and demanded endless attention. We all heaved a sigh of relief when it was time for him to go home.

'A few days later, however, we were amazed to receive the largest box of expensive chocolates we had ever seen! All sweets were strictly rationed at that time of course and coupons had to handed in before they could be bought.'

That story is backed up by a 'nipper' at the time, William Moore, who says:

'...clothes, like food, were rationed. This included bed and lined clothing. Books were issued, coupons being detached when a purchase was made. A man would probably be able to buy a jacket, vest, pants and two pairs of socks in a twelve month period. A lady similarly around one pair of sheets and pillow cases or a blanket would be allowed, if you had not used the coupons to buy towels, tea towels etc...'

Rationing was of course part of the war. It affected not just civilians but the armed forces, too. Ron Whitefield, who served in the war, remembers a poignant incident in which his Commanding Officer wanted to teach the men under his command a vital lesson. Over to you, Ron Goldstein:[81]

'On one occasion he told us that he had been annoyed to hear of his troops complaining about the size of their portions at mealtimes. He went on to say that civilians back in England were still having to live on very restricted rations and, to shame us all, he was having set up at the entrance to the dining hall a table on which would be the civilian's rations for a week. Having delivered his sermon for the week, we were then dismissed to our duties.

'The very next day the whole regiment was abruptly summoned on an unscheduled parade to be faced by an apoplectic CO. Some had stolen the civilians' rations for the week!

'I can't remember what terrible punishment he meted out to us for this heinous behaviour, but I still remember the colour of his face when he made his announcement.'

Rationing, it appears, affected everyone, including kids. William Moor also recollects how this aspect of war

---

81 Ron Goldstein, WW2 People's War. Courtesy BBC.

George Korankye

life appeared to have at times embarrassing effects. Talking about rationing, he informs us:

'A schoolboy would only possess one pair of short trousers for school, one pair for Sunday best, and one pair worn out for playing in. Boys starting school, or old ones of a nervous disposition, who wet their trousers had them dried out by the fireplace at night and were humiliated at school next day as the body heat and enclosed room heat generated the acidity of the urine. Girls were in a better situation as knickers were easily and readily changed. My personal humiliation was having to wear nurses' cut-down, thick black stockings when I had no socks.'

Now someone would at this point interject that if a child had 'wet himself' why did the parents not just put their clothes into a washing machine, pour in biological powder, turn on the 40 degree cycle, put them into the dryer and 'hey presto'? The poor child would have been gleaming white, ready to face another day at school. If you had to ask this question, it would appear that you were ignorant of the conditions prevailing at the time.

There are things we classify as necessities today that that generation would have considered luxuries.

The point is that when we talk of sacrifices being made during those war years we automatically - and rightly so - think of the human sacrifices. It is right and proper to see things in this manner.

However, we must not also forget other sacrifices people made, those that do not readily come to mind to us in the 21st century.

Some of these ancillary or secondary sacrifices also had a devastating effect on people's lives. Having one pair of trousers today would be very rare.

162

Going back to women's roles. Most industries accepted women, including the railways. However, there was still a dogged resistance to their being employed. George Glover, now over 80 years old, remembers when he was a young firer living in Bolton and had to work with women. He put in writing:

'The minimum firing age was 18 in the first years of the war, but by prior conscription and bomb damage and casualties the age was later reduced to 17…although females carried out almost every other aspect of war time duties, and although employed as porters, signal women, shunters and guards, etc, they were never ever employed as engine crews. Anyway, at the depot there were two scallywags called "Fred and Harold (F & H)", the terrible twin.'

George continues, 'There were four females who worked at Plodder Sheds at Farmworth Bolton called Ivy, Lilly and two shed sweepers, Margaret and Rose. They had their own small cabin. They used to use the main mess room for their morn and afternoon breaks, etc, but the shed cleaners (M & R) foolishly left their tea and sugar brew jar and their two mugs on top of the cupboard in the mess room (for convenience) but not without the scallywags noticing.

'They went to the nearby shop and bought a full packet of *EX-LAX*, which were chocolate constipation laxatives. They crushed the whole packet and put it into Margaret and Rose's tea and sugar jar and shook it up etc…as Margaret and Rose had approximately three brews daily. It was *NO SURPRISE* the following morning to notice BAGS under their eyes and to note *DURING THE DAY* that their brushes, shovels and barrows were *STOOD IDLY VACATED* for many periods during the day…thanks to the pranks of the stupid scallywags' (George's italics).

Women became valuable in another field, at customs checkouts. Today, the drug mule is a well-known profession and customs have adopted all manner of techniques to catch perpetrators. No one would question a man searching a woman. This was not always the case, as newly declassified documents show the government was in a quandary.

This was because of a reputed incident whereby a woman of 'high class' had been searched by a male customs officer. Well, there were consternations all round and for the sake of the peace it was decided the prudent thing to do was to let women through without searching them.

Human nature being what it is, there will always be one or two who will take advantage of any lax in security measures. They will interpret kindness as weakness.

It soon became clear that drastic action was needed by Customs to stem the flow of illicit contraband into the UK. Men could not be used, so invariably they turned to women.

Once they proved their metal they were accepted with open arms. In fact one of the reasons women were so successful at catching potential smugglers was their ability 'go places' men found it difficult to reach.[82]

Another benefit of the war can thus be seen in that, as women gained equality, they became adept at imitating the daring and underworld deeds of their male counterparts. It was not only the government but also those in the medical profession who saw first hand the

---

82 Courtesy National Archives (2008) ref: CUST 106/43/1-2.

benefits of humour, long before current research established humour could be a weapon in fighting diseases and illnesses. Evelyn White, a nurse relocated from Birmingham to help in London in 1940, recounts in her own words:

'On night duty we would have to put the beds into the centre of the ward to prevent flying glass from coming in from falling bombs. The patients, who were nearly all cockneys, were wonderful. *GREAT SENSE OF HUMOUR.* No matter how ill they were feeling, they'd always get out of bed and help us to push the beds into the middle of the ward.

'There was great fellowship. The air-raid shelters in the hospital grounds filled with water, so we couldn't use them, so we converted the x-ray department into a large air-raid shelter. They sandbagged it, they put in wooden pillars. If we were on duty at night, we would bring our mattresses over to the nurses' home, spread them out on the floor and spend the night in the x-ray room, which was well protected, we hoped, from direct hits.

'*I CAN'T EVER REMEMBER LAUGHING SO MUCH AS I DID IN THOSE DAYS.* I think perhaps it was a reaction, but *IT WAS GREAT FUN.* There was a sense of fellowship: "We're all in it together - we've got to pull together"[83] (author's italics).

Blackouts were measures put into place to protect the public. Did it produce any memorable incidents? Read further exploits of those who were there in the next chapter.

---

83 *Lest We Forget: Forgotten Voices from 1914-1945* by Max Arthur (2007) p195. Courtesy Random House Publishing.

Chapter 7

The Blackouts and Home Front

'If its sanity you are after there is no
recipe like laughter'
Henry Elliot (1817-1907)

The UK government, after declaration of hostilities in WW2, initially feared that gas attacks by the Germans were a very real possibility. The spectre of gas warfare began in WW1 and, although the scientists came up with ways of dealing with this noxious weapon by the end of the war, there was a belief that this 'German Barbarian' would resort to this form of subterfuge. They could not be trusted to play by the 'rules of war' - after all, they were not British.

What people, especially those in authority, forgot was that the 'Hun' also suffered tremendous casualties. It was not the deaths that were horrendous, but the ways in which people died that provoked such a cautious approach to the deployment of gas on the battlefields.

A slow, painful, lingering and agonising death awaited those unfortunate enough to be caught in its vapour after its release. Death was not quick like a bullet, it did not normally leave dreadful blast wounds like those that a bomb or shrapnel from an explosion would inflict as a calling card.

Consequently, by mutual consent a kind of 'gentleman's agreement' prevailed. Tacitly all the warring parties did not deploy gas as a weapon during

167

WW2. Silently and innocuously it was shelved and put on the 'back burner', ready to re- ignited with vengeance if the other side dared to break this covert agreement and deploy it.

All sides - friends, foes, neutrals and the undecided - reluctantly learned the painful lesson and consequences of its use by applying the proverb 'once bitten twice shy'. The images of men choking, gasping for breath, blindly being led one in front of another to a safe place, were firmly etched in the minds of decision makers of all the warring countries. Governments were prepared to sacrifice their men but they wanted them to die with dignity, honour, bravely and, if at all possible, quickly.

To safeguard its huge 'human investments' Whitehall, in a pre-emptive mood, even went a step further than adopting the age old maxim of 'once bitten twice shy code'; it added to that saying 'prevention is better than cure'.

What made this gas so dangerous was, although deadly, it had a kind of attractive aroma. Like the mythical Greek sirens enticing ships to the rocks.[84]

Have you ever been in a situation where you instinctively knew it was dangerous but for some perverse reason you were attracted to that danger? That was the effect the gas had. To get an idea of this 'temptation', please note the words of Corporal Jack Dillion of the Tank Corps in 1917:

---

84 In Greek mythology, the Sirens were three dangerous bird-women, who were depicted as temptresses. They resided on a mythical island surrounded by submerged cliffs and rocks. Any sailors who veered towards their island were then decoyed by these mythical Sirens by music and their soothing enticing female voices, which were so pleasant that the sailors could not resist and subsequently became casualties. Many readers will recall seeing these sirens in the film *Jason and the Argonauts* (1963).

'At Passchendale the smells were very marked and very sweet. Very sweet indeed. The first smell one got when going up the track was a very sweet smell which you only later found out was the smell of decaying bodies – men and mules. After that you got the smell of chlorine gas, which was like the sort of pear drops you'd known as a child. In fact the stronger and more attractive the pear-drop smell became, the more gas there was and the more dangerous it was. When you were walking up the track a shell dropping into the mud stirring it all up would release a great burst of smells.'[85]

Saddam Hussein (1937-2006) was later to resurrect the use of gas in the Iran-Iraq Wars (1980-1988) later in the 20th century. Beaming images live from Iraq straight to TV sets, newsreels brought to millions around the globe the terrifying aftermath of a gas attack against the Kurds. In their living rooms people could see for themselves its toxic and silent nature.

A generation fed on a diet of superficial TV shows, which had never seen firsthand a dead body except on the small or large screen, now witnessed immediately the insidious nature of a gas attack. It must have brought back terrible memories to those whose family members had been totally devastated by this weapon which many thought was defunct, consigned to the scrapheap, never to rear its ugly head, but now brought back to life.

Gas was now seen by a new generation, protected from witnessing and experiencing its ghastly consequences. In fact, one of the reasons given for the Gulf War was that Saddam Hussein was developing

---

85 *Forgotten Voices of The Great War: A new history of world war two in the words of the men and women who were there* by Max Arthur (2003) p233. Courtesy Random House Publishing.

'weapons of mass destruction' and one of these 'weapons' was mustard gas, whose effects could be clearly seen during the Iran–Iraq wars and WW1. With the legacy of previous attacks, a vivid memory in many minds, a 'zero tolerance' option was easy to sell to the general public.

The humour surrounding gas attacks was taken up by the cartoonists, partly because a massive attack failed to come about. It can be argued that maybe if people had been subjected to its poisonous 'fruitage' perhaps it would have been deemed to be in bad taste to make fun of people 'coughing their guts out'.

'Certainly the soldiers on the front never experienced gas attacks, making it acceptable to write poems of what could have been.

An interesting story was that of Annie Howell[86] who took a job making gas masks during WW1. You have to say that her naivety is indeed amusing. Working in this factory you will never guess what she says:

'The war never sunk into me, that the war meant they'd got to kill each other to win. It never entered my head. I just knew it was a gas mask. One day, I said to this girl, "This gas masks, what's it for - where do they put the gas?"

"Oh, no," she said, "they don't put the gas in it. The Germans throw gas bombs over and they gas the men."

"Oh," I said. I was a bit ignorant in lots of ways.'

Annie Howell was not alone in being ignorant of the uses of a gas mask. Even in WW2 Doris Scott, a civilian in East London, said:

---

86 *Women At War* (2002) Courtesy Imperial War Museum Ref 000613/08.

Die Laughing – War Humour

'Thought it was awfully funny - although I suppose I shouldn't say that in a war - but when the warning went, there was a chappie who lived at the end of the street. He was under the impression that as soon as the warning went, that he had to put on his gas mask. He did this over and over again, running through the streets with it on. We had been told only to use the gas mask if we heard rattles, and that the normal warning was for getting into your shelter. It was very funny.'

William Maylam's poem reflects the attitude of soldiers at the time about gas.

The Gas Rhyme

If you get a choking feeling
And a smell of musty hay
You can bet your bottom dollar
That there's **PHOSGENE** on the way

Or the smell of bleaching powder
And a suffocating scene
Means the enemy you're meeting
Is the gas that's called **CHLORINE**

When your eye begins a twitching
And for tears you cannot see
Tisn't mother peeling onions
But a dose of C.A.P.

And then that smell of pear drops
Or nail polish they say
Isn't children sucking sweeties
But that tear gas K.S.K

Onions, horseradish or garlic
Is a smell that hits you hard
Though some say it smells on onions
It's that deadly gas **MUSTARD**

Should you smell a bitter sweetness
With the tears not so intense
Then it's B.B.C. you're sniffing
Its persistence is immense

And the smell of sweet geraniums
Though quite pleasant in a bed
Do not be misled in wartime
For it's LEWISITE instead

PERSISTANT GASES:- B.B.C – K.S.K.
MUSTARD and LEWISITE
NON PERSISTANT:- CHLORINE – C.A.P.
PHOSGENE – D.A. – D.M. – D.C.

In Britain, getting your gas mask was just like collecting your ration book. It was a 'must have' item of the day; no respectable 'hoodie' would be seen without their gas masks. Mickey Mouse was drafted in from Hollywood to appeal to children to see the necessity of wearing their masks. William Moore remembers living in his village:

'…on foot at the age of five, walking five miles in all weathers with school satchel and meat paste, jam or even lard sandwiches would not be acceptable today. A gas mask would also have to be carried daily, also identity cards, excusable once in a week if forgotten. Then you were sent home to fetch any of the three items and return to school, kept in at play time to do lines so one did not often forget.'

William Moore goes on to relate 'child abuse is brought to justice these days, thankfully, if found out. It went on in my school days, sadly never being known about'.

The media saw a fertile ground for humour once gas masks were issued, treating the whole episode with unbelievable joviality owing to the fact everyone possessed one. This became a good way for cartoonists and their like to cheer up the general public and to help them 'lighten up', yes to see the hilarious side of what could have been a very terrifying ordeal.

According to Heather Crook of Preston, daughter of Eric Crook (1917-2007) mentioned earlier:

'...was born in a workhouse, and brought up in an orphanage from the age of 7. At 14 he was sent to be a live-in farm labourer, a job that he was doing when war broke out.

'He went to Italy. He was trained to place devices on tanks to blow them up. Got hit by a bazooka, shrapnel went into his face. Terrible burns and a cut from his brow in between his eyes, along the side of his nose, across his lips and down his chin. Flown home and spent a long time in hospital, convalescing. Had to have glycerine wiped on his lips to stop them fusing together.'

Barbara Chapman, now an ex-school teacher, recollects:

'...I can vividly remember taking my ration book to the sweet shop in East Cowes, having to reach up on tiptoe to put it and my money on the counter to get some delicious home-baked tin toffee - broken up by a hammer. Health and Safety wouldn't allow it today!'[87]

When you think of it, there was so much 'boo ha ha' in 2006 about identity cards and how we are all reduced to numbers by the government. However, comparing 2008 to 1939, it would appear that no one during WW2 looked at things in that manner. ID cards were not viewed as stripping people of their personality or reducing them to a faceless person in a crowd.

The whole concept is reminisce of the 1960s television program 'The Prisoner' where Patrick McGoohan, playing the part of a prisoner, is given the number 'Six' in a vain attempt by his captors, who try to strip him of his identity. He then goes on record by uttering those famous words that have come to be a tag line for those fighting conformity: 'I am not a number, I am a free man'.[88]

To the left and in the following page are two examples of Air Raid Wardens' training in the use of gas masks.[89]

They were rather unflattering to wear, but serve a purpose.

---

87 Barbara says she wants '...as many people as possible to know about their history/heritage - hence the websites I run.

They can be found at www.lgchronicle.net/ and www.lgchronicle.net/WW2.html

88 'The Prisoner' was a science fiction television programme. It is about an ex-British secret agent who finds himself imprisoned by a secretive power in a small village and who then tries to establish his identity. He is stripped of his individuality and given the number '6'.

89 Courtesy www.cyberheritage.co.uk

SOMEBODY SHOUTED GAS! – AND SMITH
FORGOT TO TAKE HIS PIPE OUT !!!

If you happen to be a certain generation, you will no doubt remember the 'Winter of Discontent' or the 'Three Day Week'.[90]

Blackouts were introduced with the sole aim of thwarting the German navigators and bomb aimers. After curfew, no lights were to be shone, curtains were to be drawn shut, window boards closed, street lamps were to be extinguished and car lamps darkened. In fact, not a glimmer of light was to be seen, thus denying the enemy aircrafts any idea of their location while on their bombing runs. Kathy Robinson of Peacehaven in East Sussex lived

90 This term was used to describe the 'Winter of Discontent' (1978–1979), when there were widespread strikes by trade unions who were demanding above-inflation wage increases. The strikes caused considerable problems leading to food shortages and power cuts. Or you may recollect the Three-Day Week from 1 January until 7 March 1974 which was put in place by the then Conservative Government to preserve power supplies. The use of electricity by commercial firms was limited, leading to power cuts throughout the UK.

in Hertfordshire at the time of WW2. She remembers a funny incident which she relates:

'Train windows were covered a kind of mesh to prevent glass splinters and injuries during air raids. A poster on a train from Liverpool Street London to Hertford read:

"Pardon us for our suggestion, this Stuff is here for your protection".

'A hole had been scraped on the protective covering and at the bottom of the poster some wag had written:

"We thank you for the information but cannot see the blasted station".'

During blackouts coupled with air raids, many must have been absolutely petrified. In the distance, or perhaps even close by, would be the loud booms of anti-aircraft guns, bombs dropped from the skies, houses shaking violently with rage as if they were complaining about their treatment. They stood silently, bearing the full might of the onslaught with a dignified spirit, watching and waiting staunchly for the return of their occupants.

In addition, the noises of dogfights coupled with the loud droning of aeroplanes shot down or losing height due to failing engines, would turn the silence of the night into a crescendo of sounds. Living in the 21st century, when most of our experiences of war have come via courtesy of television or the cinema, it is difficult to imagine the magnitude of the sounds prevailing if a blackout was followed by an air raid.

The story of Jim Moulding[91] below needs no further input. It brings home the destruction and the humour

---

91 Jim Moulding, WW2 People's War. Courtesy BBC.

beautifully. Would you not agree this person nearly died laughing?

'One amazing fact about wartime Britain was that, often amidst anxiety and danger, humour could appear as if from nowhere.

'It was in the early stages of the war that I found myself with the Fleet Air Arm in Portsmouth. How few people today really appreciate the tremendous bomb damage this city suffered during the war? So much destruction, yet the people coped with courage and no small amount of humour, a smile often just around the corner.

'On one occasion I was in an air raid shelter beneath the naval barracks parade ground, when a German landmine dropped close by. After clambering out, the authorities decided that the new recruits should march to South Sea, out of the way. We weren't actually marching - more like ambling through the bomb-damaged streets with not a soul in sight. Suddenly we heard a noise that seemed to be coming from a confused mass of wooden beams, bricks and rubble. It sounded like laughter.

'Two or three of us climbed over the rubble and looked down into a huge hole. There we saw an old man sitting on something, laughing loudly.

'We called down from above, "Are you alright?"

'At first we didn't get a response so we shouted louder. Eventually the old man heard us and looked up.

"Hello lads, you'll have to shout, I'm hard of hearing."
'We repeated the question.

"I'm alright," he said still laughing. "I always said these houses were Jerry built and today I've been proved right'.

177

'We looked puzzled but he continued, "I only pulled the toilet chain, there was a bang and the whole house fell down!"'

Then, as if that is hard to believe, how about this from Allan Scott: [92]

'The following account comes in a letter written by my Danish mother, Minna Scott, in 1944, to my father (then with the RAPC in Italy). My parents rented a flat in Warlingham; it was owned by a Mr and Mrs Bellatti, who lived downstairs and were the friendliest possible landlords.

'Mr Bellatti's son came for the weekend and I was invited down to tea on the veranda. The four of us were sitting comfortably sipping tea when the warning siren sounded.

Mr B: "There it goes again!!"

Young Mr B: "May I have another cup of tea please?"

Me: "How I do hate wasps. Here is one in my honey."

Mrs B: "Yes, they are a nuisance. I will get a piece of Cellophane to put over the Swiss roll." Meanwhile three bombs are rapidly approaching.

'Mr B: "That one is very near. Hadn't we better get up?"

Mrs B: "Now the cake is safe. How I do want my tea?"

Me: "Oh! Oh! Oh! That wasp is determined to sting me. Help!"

Young Mr B: "By the way, it is my wedding anniversary today; do you know, I should like to have a change of wife, pity it is not allowed."

---

92 Allan Scott, WW2 The People's War. Courtesy BBC.

Mrs B: "Oh look! You spilled the tea when you carried the tray out."

Me: "It is coming down. Look over there!"

Mr B: "Get down! Get down! It is coming!"

Young Mr B: "Why, it will fall half a mile away at least. May I have another cup of tea, please? I am still parched."

Mrs B is saying something, but owing to a colossal explosion only the tail-end of the sentence is heard.

"More bread and butter or would you rather have a piece of cake?" while Mr B is picking himself up from the lawn where he has thrown himself.

'And so it goes on and I wonder what good it can possibly do the Germans to destroy the houses of the English. Or possibly young Mr B is right when he says that Hitler's secret weapon is to ruin the digestion of the enemy by coming over at meal-times.'

Text: **'John I told you not put your clothes my side of the bed.'**

Nowadays, 'cross dressing' is an accepted form of behaviour in numerous countries. However, during the war years no man worth his salt would have been seen dead in a woman's clothes. Men dressed as women was seen as a comical anathema, not so in our politically correct day whereby this kind of hilarity is not frowned upon.

People from Scotland at times coming in for some 'tomfoolery' over the national costume of the kilt.

Lieutenant Hartwig Pohlman[93] of the German Army remembers vividly his first encounter in 1917 of the Highlanders. He said: 'We happened to catch some of the Highlanders, and it was a funny sight for us to see soldiers with kilts and naked knees.'

We are not told what the German for 'sissy' is but you can rest assured the laughs and name calling would not be worth printing. This view has not coloured, affected even influenced the 'jocks' that wear with pride what they consider their distinctive identity.

The blackout produced comical and interesting committee meetings.

On the next page is the official 'Top Secret Meeting' of the Government. Apart from figures of Armed forces that have been removed NO EDITING OF WORDS HAS TAKEN PLACE (except for removal of numerical figures).[94]

The text is mind-boggling, and makes you wonder how we have developed as a nation to where we are now in the world rankings of civilised Western nations. What follows reads like some comedy of errors text!

---

93 *Forgotten Voices of The Great War: A new history of World War Two in the words of the men and women who were there* by Max Arthur (2003) p233. Courtesy Random House Publishing.

94 Courtesy Imperial War Museum.

Cabinet War Rooms
Civilian War Readiness Planning Committee[95]

Briefing Papers

In this folder, you will find information which will help you and your colleagues to decide what to say in your report to the Committee. You should aim to prepare a clear plan of action, and to be ready to speak for about five minutes.

In that five minutes, you will:

- Describe the problem you have been asked to plan for
- Explain what you think should be done
- Give details of how you think your plans can be carried out
- Consider details of what difficulties there may be, and what should be done to overcome them.

You should be prepared to answer questions from other members of the Committee when you have finished your presentation.

Your Brief Is

How shall we prepare in case the Germans try to invade Britain?

We expect the enemy to try to invade our country. In the past, this has been difficult, thanks to the protection of the sea, but modern technology, including aeroplanes, and ships that are able to travel whatever the weather,

---

95 www.iwm.org.uk/upload/pdf/CWRWRinvasion.pdf

means that this time it is likely that the enemy will invade us, as has always happened to the other countries of Europe. In this folder is a map of Europe, which shows how much the Germans have taken already, and which countries are allied to them or have decided to be neutral. The Committee will want your advice on all kinds of matters.

Issues to consider:

- How big are our Army, Navy and Airforce? Is this enough? The government has just decided to reintroduce conscription as we did in the last war, but who should be called up?
- Do we have the forces to prevent an invasion? If not, what parts of the coast should we defend most strongly?
- Can we make some use of people who are too old, or are not needed for the regular armed forces, but who still want to help?
- Can we make sure that the German Airforce does not do too much harm to our defences?
- What about spies and traitors?
- What should we do to make our coastlines harder to attack and land on?
- If the Germans do land, how can we make sure they do not know where they are or where to go next?
- If there is a successful invasion, what should we tell the general public? Should they form a 'Resistance', and keep on fighting in undercover ways? Or should they 'collaborate', for instance by sacking Jewish people as has happened in Germany, Austria and Czechoslovakia?

182

The committee may want your advice about who should be called up:

- What is the youngest age at which men should be called? (In the last war it was 18)
- At what age should people be considered 'too old'? (In the last war, it was 41)
- What should happen to people who try to refuse to do their National Service, for instance because they do not believe in killing? In the last war, these 'conscientious objectors' were often put in prison and treated very badly. Is this the right thing to do?
- Should only men be called up? Of course women should not fight, but there are lots of jobs in the Forces which do not involve fighting. Should women be conscripted, or should we just ask them to volunteer?

Using people who are not in the Services:

Air Raid Precautions

Do we need to recruit people, full time, or part time, to deal with warnings, rescue people from bombed buildings and so on? Should they be paid, or volunteer? What should they be told to do if the invasion happens?

A Possible 'Home Guard'?

Will it be useful to have people who are not in the forces training to fight? Or is it better only to have soldiers to defend our country? If we do have such a force, should there be age limits? Is 15 too young? What is too old? 60? 70? 80?

Should people be paid for this service? Who should pay them, the government, or the local area council? Should they be paid as much as a soldier, or less?

What should be done about weapons for them? Should they use good, new weapons, like the army has, or should they just be issued with old, or sporting kinds of weapons?

Anti-Aircraft Batteries

Should these be worked by 'real' soldiers or by volunteers, or women?

The need to be near the cities, but where should they be stationed? On waste land? In parks and recreation grounds? Is there a risk that children will try to get near the guns and be in danger? What about the damage when shot-down planes crash? Is there a risk that having anti-aircraft guns will cause more attacks as the Germans try to destroy them?

Extra Information: what actually happened!

(Broadcast by Anthony Eden, Secretary of State for War On 14 May 1940 - the day the Netherlands surrendered.)

'We are going to ask you to help us in a manner which I hope will be welcome to thousands of you. Since the war began, the Government has received countless enquiries from all over the kingdom, from men of all ages, who are for one reason or another at present not engaged in military service and who wish to do something for the defence of the country. Now is your opportunity. We want large numbers of such men in Great Britain who are British subjects, between the ages of fifteen and sixty-five, to come forward now and offer their services in order to make assurance doubly sure. The name of the new force which is now to be raised will be the Local Defence Volunteers.'

(Within 24 hours over 250,000 men had volunteered, and by 30 June it was over 1,400,000; the name was soon changed to 'Home Guard'. The force was demobilised in December 1944, by which time 1,206 had died of wounds or been killed while on duty. Different anti aircraft batteries were run by different people: some by volunteers, some by men from the army, and some by women of the ATS (Auxiliary Territorial Service).)

Making sure the Luftwaffe cannot find its way
Air pilots use landmarks on the ground to work out where they are and where they are going. And it is the lights from the ground that tell them where their targets are. The Committee will want advice about how to deal with this. Would it be helpful to make all of Britain dark at night? How can this be done? You might suggest what should be done about:

Houses and flats • Shops • Streets • Street crossings • Restaurants, pubs and cafes • Railways and underground stations • Cinemas and theatres • Hospitals • Police, ambulance and fire stations

Some questions the Committee may ask are:

- What about people's personal rights? Can we order people to do certain things to their own home?

- Should the government pay for them to get the materials they need to darken their home or business?
- What will happen if restaurants, pubs and cinemas lose business because nobody knows they are there, and open? Will there be compensation?
- What about road safety? Imagine a city street, with buses and cars, but no lights!
- Who should make sure people keep to these rules? Is this extra work for the police? Will people be sent to prison for not 'blacking out'?

Spies and signposts

- Would it be wise to get rid of all the signposts and street and station names, so that Germans, if they arrive by parachute, cannot tell where they are or where they are going? What are the problems with this for ordinary people, postmen, visitors etc? Who should do it, and where should the money come from?
- Should we warn the general public to look out for spies and German troops in disguise? Can we think of some test words that German people find difficult to say? Then the public can be advised to trick strangers into saying one of them!
- Should we imprison people who are suspected of backing the Nazis, even if we have no proof? The Committee will want your advice on where to put them and how to treat them

- If there are spies, they may learn a lot by listening to people who are just chatting in shops and pubs and bus queues. You need to tell the Committee whether you think this is a big risk, and what should be done to stop it. Is it possible to control what people say to their family and friends? Should people be warned to 'keep quiet'?

***

The Home Guards also came in for some rib tickling fun. These were people usually considered either too old or too young for active duties but who nevertheless wanted to contribute and to do their bit for the war effort.

What should be the duties of these fine muscle-toned individuals, or what were they actually to do? After much brainstorming, their grandiose or noble role was to 'defend the country in the country'. This group would be trained and formed into a 'lean, mean, fighting machine' able to take on any invader, any infidel, that dared breach the defences of their honourably country. Once their remit was established the question arose as to their proper name which, of course, should reflect their duties. Their name would be 'The Local Defence Force', later renamed as the Home Guard (1940-1944).

The Home Guard became a household name. The nickname 'Dad's Army' became synonymous not for 'those who are about to die salute you, Caesar' but 'those too old to die salute you, Caesar'. Look at the drawing on the following page by Nicholas Bentley (1907-1978). You will notice the word 'Eh'. The expression is intended to poke fun at the effectiveness of such a force if the Germans were to invade Britain.

187

George Korankye

Text: **'Eh!'**

Observe that a German paratrooper is shown. Why is this scene very funny? You have to laugh at someone with an old antiquated shotgun who has impaired hearing and failing eyesight due to old age trying to stop a young German paratrooper in their prime, armed to the teeth, creeping stealthily upon them.

But that's not all. Can you visualise this 'Home Guard' trying to stop him? In fact, the old shotgun was a dig at the government being unable to provide enough weapons for this 'fighting force'.

Really nothing has in actual fact altered. No government has an infinite amount of monies to spend on equipment, whether it is at peace or war. There will always be a trade off; hard decisions will have to be made when all the different branches of the armed forces come cup in hand and jostle for funds to enable them to have the latest equipment.

To further exacerbate the efforts of any determined German paratrooper, a brilliant plot was hatched whereby all the signposts from the roads would be taken out of the ground, meaning that if the worst did happen then the enemy would be totally confused, unable to negotiate his way around his newly invaded country.

Recently declassified materials available from the National Archives paint a true picture of 'Dads Army'. It shows that all the points made were accurate.[96]

The recruitment drive certainly worked. Within a few hours of the government requesting help from volunteers to thwart a German invasion, it was reported over 250,000 men had offered their services. But these men were short of weapons so the government once again resorted to the power of the media and requested that, in a public show of support for this new band, weapons not in use by the public should be donated. This resulted in 20,000 weapons of various sorts being surrendered for this new 'elite force'.

'Sir, During the last war—'

Text: **'Sir, during the last war.'**

---

96 Courtesy National Archives (2008) CAB 120/240 and WO 199/3249.

Interestingly this force was not only armed with antiquated shotguns, they also had pitchforks, spears, coshes, crossbows, broom handles, crowbars, garden pikes and even a drainpipe with a blade attached to it. Presumably some of these men were going to club the Germans to death, others were going to be like Zulu warriors and use their spears to deadly effect. They even lacked basic uniforms.

The name 'Dad's Army' derived basically from the fact that it was not just their ages, but that most of these men were old WW1 veterans, truly past the bloom of youth. The cartoon above shows the problems the government had in trying to equip these men. No wonder they became a joke and fodder for cartoonists and the public alike. It did not go unnoticed even by very small children.

Mark Northolt from Leyland wrote:

'My story from summer 1944 involves an incident in which I took part but cannot remember, which my father used to tell. I was being evacuated from London to Leicester as the menace from VIs (doodlebugs) was increasing. The blackout was of course in operation and all station names (and signposts) had been obliterated in order to hamper and frustrate any German invasion. As the train pulled into each station, people strained to recognise where they were. I was around 7½ years old at the time, and clearly proud of my newly acquired reading skill. As the train pulled into yet another station, my high-pitched little voice shouted confidently, "I know where we are. This is gentleman station!" The carriage erupted in mirth.'

What Mr Northolt (1936-) said in conversation in addition to his letter above was that places were pitch black, nothing was recognisable, and that all he could make out were words such as the toilets signs 'ladies' and 'gentlemen', even adverts like 'bisto'.

Mr Northolt is not the only one to have childhood recollections. Brian Heaton from Cheshire writes:

'At the end of the Second World War I was 8 years old, and like many we didn't travel very far from home. On one of the occasions when my auntie visited us for a short holiday, she decided to take my mother, brother and myself to New Brighton for the day (holiday resort). We lived in Eccles, Manchester, at the time and this day out meant going by train to Liverpool, and ferry to New Brighton. Somewhere along the way we came across and went into the fish market, a very dark and gloomy place. Like only a young child can do, I asked my auntie in a very loud whisper the following:

"Auntie Marjorie, is this the black market?"

'Needless to say we hurried on our way without comment.'

Don't you admire the childhood simplicity? Does it not evoke memories of your own innocence? The funny thing is, why had Auntie Marjorie kept silent? Perhaps she was a frequent visitor to a clandestine black market? Poor Brian must have heard this mentioned before but, in his innocence, he misunderstood what kind of place it was.

Did you notice, too, that Brian went to Brighton by train? Is it possible he could have been a passenger on a train fired by George Glover from Plodders sheds in Bolton?

Talking of George, he relates a story about two scallywags, or 'the terrible twins' as he calls them:

191

'…whenever the two were on duty there was trouble. One of their duties was to see that every engine arriving was serviced, fired, coaled, watered and stabled in order of departures. There was a "turn" - a person who turned trains in the opposite direction - called Bill Entwistle, who had a voice like a foghorn. He did not go to the usual mess canteen, but used the special turner's hut with its stovepipe fire, a small table and three seat-type lockers which he used for forty winks when possible.

'On the night in question, Bill and his mate were exceptionally busy and late, and so foolishly he asked the mad DUO (the scallywags) if they would put some coal on his cabin fire ready for his meal break, a fact they did but amongst the coal they also placed two fog signal detonators on the top layer of coal.

'When it was time for his brew and butties, Bill got comfy after his meal and lay on the three lockers for his usual 40 winks, but no sooner had he lied down than a couple of loud explosions rocked his cabin as the fog signals exploded, bringing down *YEARS OF SOOT – DUST* and whatever, plus ashes from the fire and leaving *BILL COVERED*[97] and dashing outside swearing at the top of his voice with *THREATS* to the two scallywags. But he looked hilarious with his jet black face looking as though he was ready to drop to one knee and sing AL JOLSON'S "MAMMY".[98]

---

97 See cartoon of this incident by Jordon Krawczyk.

98 Performing some of his films using blackface makeup has been a bone of contention among many critics. What these critics forget is that this was a theatrical convention employed by many entertainers at that time. In fact it was still used in Britain in the popular television programme 'The Black and White Minstrel Show' (1958-78) which ran for 20 years and at its peak attracted 18 million viewers. Acting required the putting on of a variety of makeup, especially if other

'However, I don't think the hospital patients would have appreciated it *AS HIS VOICE MUST HAVE AWAKENED ALMOST THE WHOLE HOSPITAL.*

'I blame him for being so foolish as to trust the *DUO* in the first place... (HE never asked them again!*).'* (Italics and capitals George's.) [99]

George went on to write a poem about this incident, which is on the following page.

---

nationalities were being portrayed. Al Jolson was unique in the sense that he became the most famous entertainer to use blackface makeup.

99 If we use the standards of the 21st century where by and large equality in acting prevails among the different races, we may be offended by referring to a 'Black Face'. However, looking at things from the viewpoint of the early 20th century some have suggested his black face was just a prop, a practice routinely used by other performers. Others claim that by using this method Al Jolson could perform incognito and therefore his actions were not racially motivated.

George Korankye

Shed Turners Nightmare

With the last engine stabled
Between Midnight and two,
It was time for Bill Entie
To partake of a brew.

So entering into
His small nearby hut,
With its nice cosy fire
And its door warmly shut.
After finishing his drink
And the butties he did choose
His mind wandered off
To a forty winks snooze.
So stretching full length
On the three locker bed
And using his coat
To pillow his head.
But! Before he dropped off
There was a mighty explosion
From the little hot stove
With the fog signal 'dets
Causing commotion.

So rushing outside,
With face black and clammy
He gave an impression
Of Al Jolson's Mammy
But I don't think the staff
At the hospital close by
Did thank his loud voice
For the lack of shut eye.

Die Laughing – War Humour

The poem well described what happened that day. Imagine an 80-year-old man sitting at home by his coal fire, recollecting with clarity what happened all those years ago.

An interesting point to show the paranoia is that the government, in order to deceive these 'barbarians' and to throw their armed forces into total confusion as to where they were, removed all signs, dug them out then put them to good military use.

These super-fit Germans, upon either parachuting or landing in 'Blighty', would not know the way to London, Manchester, Liverpool, Edinburgh or anywhere in Britain.[100] Therefore, unable to navigate their way around their newly conquered satellite state, they would abandon any plans of occupation, jump back into their boats and return home in disgrace. That would teach those blighters.

Text: **'I'll never tell nobody where anywhere is.'**
Artist: George Sherriff Sherwood
[101]

"I'll tell nobody where anywhere is."

---

100 The thought of paratroopers dropping from the sky was a threat that never really happened except, of course, in the film *The Eagle has Landed* (1976). It is alleged that this preposterous plan to capture Churchill and bring him to Germany was encouraged by the daring rescue of Adolph Hitler's then fellow dictator, Benito Mussolini, from prison. The whole rescue was carried out by the charismatic leader Otto Skorzen (1908-1975).

101 *Punch* magazine, 24 July 1940.

Home guards, it can be seen, were a regular reservoir of jokes and anecdotes.

Then of course there was the Land Army, which was conceived in WW1 and later repeated in WW2. Women were the primary target as most of the farm workers had either joined up or were conscripted. How was their lot? Surprisingly they too came in for some rib tickling fun. Of course the poor farmer's wife saw them as a threat to their men folk. Why? The basic reason was that the clothes of that time were considered not morally fit or 'proper' for decent women. The fashion at that time was long skirts, corsettes and clothes designed to keep women covered up.

It was impractical to wear long skirts or corsettes while shovelling hay or cleaning out a barn full of the leftovers from cows and all the other farm stock, and don't forget the health and safety aspects. These clothes could easily be caught up in farm machinery causing unnecessary death, mutilation or bring premature disabilities. The obvious answer was to change the way that women dressed. This of course brought looks of disgust.

Annie Edwards'[102] story provides considerable insight into the way clothes had to change because of the circumstances a person found themselves in. She relates candidly how, in 1914, she was in service, in Pulborough. With the outbreak of war she joined the Red Cross. Then, in 1915, she saw a poster for the Land Army. She continues:

'I had to have three references. So I went to Canon Baggley's wife and asked her if she would sign. She said

---

[102] *Women At War* (2002). Courtesy Imperial War Museum Ref: 000740/15.

she couldn't say anything bad about me at all. She admired me in every way of my life, excepting she objected to me dressing like a man and it's going to spoil me. Because in those days that's the first time a woman, a female, ever wore trousers, breeches or anything. I had my skirts right down. Mustn't show your ankle.

'She said, "What are you going to wear?" "Oh," I said, "breeches," because I'd already been to Worthing for the outfit. Oh, she was against that.

'But the Canon said that breeches would alter me, and that I was a good girl because I was in the choir. So in the finish she said, "As much as I dislike doing it, I will do it."

'Well, she couldn't do nothing else. So she signed it. And the doctor signed it. And my lady, where I was cook, she signed it. They hoped it wouldn't alter my life. I joined up. Well, they said, "you have been accepted in the Land Army and we have found you a farm to do your six weeks training. And it's down at Chichester".

'My mum was against that. "We've brought you up so strict. And do you know that's a barrack town soldiers?" She didn't like that. I said I didn't go with soldiers. I hadn't been with nobody. Father said, "Good," because there was more money." I said I could send some money home. It all helped because children kept coming. Times were hard.

'The first week I come down to my billet, down to the farm here, an old lady stood over there. I was the first land girl she saw and she looked up through her glasses. She said, "Huh! Neither a man or a woman." I never had a long skirt on. Sort of a red-khaki breeches, you know, not exactly khaki but a bit darker than khaki, bit on the dark red side. We didn't like it at first.

'It made us sore. It was rough. There was rough inside. There weren't proper seams. Now, the inside was raw. And of course you wore your underclothes. That helped a bit. But it did hurt in different places and under your knee, until you got used to it.

'The first year then, I was out in the field, harvest time and wet through with sweat, wet through, right through this and all. In those days our corsets were severe, all steel bones and they got nasty. And when I went up in the hayloft and I took them off and close to the farm there was an outside lavatory, where they was emptied about every third year or something. I went and folded them and took them there. And from that day to this I never wore them.'

Air raids were another frightening episode of war time. It would be hard to imagine that there could be anything more comical to recall than bombs falling 'willy nilly' from the skies, or leaving a shelter not knowing whether your house would be upright or not.

Most houses were heated by coal, which required taking the ashtray out every night. Can you imagine the mess there would be if you were taking out the ashtray one windy evening and there was a sudden gust of wind? You were quite likely to get a mouthful of good old coal dust and good whiff of coal dirt up your nose. It became acceptable to look forward to a major clean up of the furniture and dusting off 'stoor' from all the furniture after an air raid.

Elsie Hodgkin's memory of an air raid night goes like this:

'We had been told that when the air-raid warning sounded, we should make towards a middle wall of the house because it was the strongest place and least likely to collapse.

'One night, I was at my grandparents' house when the siren sounded. My granddad (who suffered gun shock from serving in the first world war) was an insurance collector and was writing up his accounts, for which he always used pen and ink (no ball points in those days). We all ran to the wall, but Granddad turned back - why? *TO PUT THE TOP BACK ON HIS INK BOTTLE, BECAUSE HE SAID – "SHE (Grandma) WILL KILL ME IF IT SPILLS ON THE TABLE!"*

'On that occasion, a bomb dropped half a mile from the house and several windows were shattered - but there was no ink on the table!' (italics Elise's).

David Turnnbull from Northumberland thinks he knows why the punch line for the end of a joke is 'boom, boom'. He relates as follows:

'You've probably heard this one before. One night a comedian was on stage somewhere in London. By sheer chance the timing at the end of each joke coincided with the firing of the heavy guns on the Western Front in France/Belgium. So he would crack a joke and at the end of each punchline the gun sound would come - boom, boom. He started saying "boom, boom", at the end of each joke punchline. Jimmy Tarbuck still uses this today. He cracks jokes and follows the punchline by saying "boom, boom".'

Anytime you are invited onto a team for a quiz you are now fully conversant with the knowledge that 'boom, boom' originated in the First World War.

George Korankye

Today traffic wardens are the bane of members of society. Some feel that they have become overzealous in their application of the law. In parts of the UK they are called the 'enforcers'.

Although some treat them disrespectfully, others have concocted jokes of various hues and shades about them showing the comical, at times farcical, side of their decisions. Well, this thought is nothing new. During the war, one cartoonist in *Punch* drew a picture which captured the same spirit in Air Raid Wardens (ARW).

You will see a carton on the following page which reflects the pedantic attitude of an ARW.

"In any case you're well over the white line."

Text: **'In any case you are well over the white line.'**[103]

---

103 *Punch*, 4 December 1940.

" I reckon I'd sleep much better if I knew what time the first train comes through."

Text: **'I reckon I'd sleep much better if I knew what time the first train comes through.'**[104]

" There's bound to be a Servants' annex somewhere, Trubshaw! "

Also, because no one knew when the all clear would sound, people could literally spend all night underground. This drew humorous attention.

Text: **'There's bound to be a Servants' annex somewhere, Trubshaw.'**[105]

Although the drawings may bring a smile to our faces, it was not far from the truth. Many living today may find

---

104 Langdon.
105 Fenwick.

the scene absurd. Why, these things only happened during the Victorian era in the days of Jane Austen. The people we automatically think of are Darcy in *Pride Prejudice*. But before we dismiss this cartoon, think of the words of Mrs Wells, from Swanley in Kent, who actually lived through these times. She penned the words below, which are printed unedited. She relates:

'I am eighty now and do not expect to live for ever! I hope you find the following tales of interest, in particular the first one which explains the different worlds the social classes occupied.

'During the war I was sixteen years old and had been fortunate to be recommended for a job in Unilever House, Blackfriars. (One had to be personally recommended by existing or past employees to be employed by such an exalted company, however lowly the position!)

'My wages were 17s-6d per week and this was not sufficient for me to afford a normal fare. However, in those days one could purchase a workingman's ticket which enabled you to travel cheaply so long as your train arrived at the London terminal before 8.15am. In my case, from Swanley to Blackfriars it cost 1s-2½ d per day.

'It was common practice to go into the ticket office on arrival at Swanley in the evening and purchase one's ticket for the following morning. Unfortunately one could not do this on a Sunday evening as the office was closed. Therefore, on Monday mornings the ticket office would be crowded with people queuing up at the two available windows. One very miserable, dark and wet winter morning we were all there, not saying much as most of us were exhausted with the war, etc. I perked up somewhat when I realised I was standing behind a very tall, handsome, young naval officer. Everything about him was brand new and squeaky clean and he was probably not long out of his cadetship.

'The depressing queues continued shuffling toward the ticket hatch and each person would mumble "Workman's to London, please".

'When it became the naval officer's turn, he said in a very loud, upper crust voice you could cut with a knife, "A first class workman's ticket to London"! Stunned silence, then roars of laughter while it was explained to him that although officers had to travel first class, they could not do it on a workman's ticket.

'He took all the banter in good heart fortunately and, because we were all mindful of the duties he would have to do and the dangerous future he had, he went with everyone's blessing and cries of "good luck mate" from the men and "Godspeed" from the women.

'I often wonder whether he survived the war, as we lost so many of our beautiful (in every sense) young men. I do hope so.'

This pre-occupation with class runs through all levels of society, even down to our era. We think of the classic 'Frost Report' (1966-1967) sketch about social class. This programme was later to feature as a launch pad for the famous *Monty Python* series.

Let's also not forget who was in the air raid shelters with their parents. Countless 'young yins' spent hours underground. The mind boggles as to what they did, cooped up like chickens underground. The answers may well be what have been found on the walls of some air raid shelters. True, they are not Banksy's, but they do show the way that the war affected their growing minds. There is a saying about 'idle hands' ...

Below, Hermann Göring (1912-1945). Courtesy Cyberimage

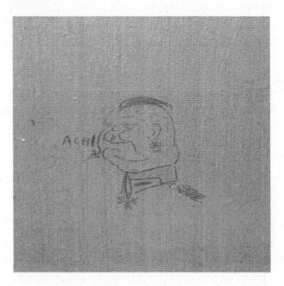

Below, HIENEKEIL Aeroplane

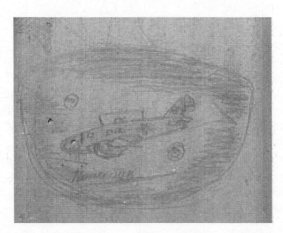

The two previous images are WW2 graffiti found in the Underground Air Raid Shelter at Sutton High School and also the shrub verge at Lower Street at Plymouth by schoolchildren from primary to grammar age.

They are a stunning window into the past and give us an opportunity to see if things have changed much. We could change those images for Osama bin Laden and other leading terrorist figures, and then we would be bang up to date.

The pictures are of a German HIENEKEIL Aeroplane and Goring, both courtesy of Cyberimage.

The Home Guard were always at the ready, like true Boy Scouts willing to help, come rain or shine. In fact, they would literally travel through the pouring rain to assist anyone. Over to you, David Turnbull:

'A Home Guard man was bicycling to the nearest town one night when it started to rain. He is supposed to have continued his journey and gone to the meeting, only to announce that he could not attend the meeting as it was raining and he was wet.'

Now would you not say that that's the 'bulldog' spirit coming out? He was determined that if he could not make it to the meeting 'by gum' he would turn up and say 'I am sorry all, but I could not make it because it was raining'.

Let's not forget the women, they too did not forget their position and seemed to carry on this ingrained class structure.

Of course, this was picked up on by the public and repeated in poems such as the one sent in by Mrs Carling of Milnathort, who was given the scrapbook of Mrs Francis Leckie (1919-2007) by her daughters:

George Korankye

His Girl's an Officer

We're billeted in this little town, we can't avoid a
meeting,
Yet in the street we can't exchange the merest little
greeting:
I watch her walk towards me - boy! Could anything be
cuter?
I holler 'Hiya, baby!'- then remember to salute 'er!

His
Girl's
An
Officer !

When going to the flicks the situation's more
fantastic,
We can't go in together - retribution would be drastic:
So I go in before her (Margaretta doesn't mind),
And, just like Mary's little lamb, she follows on
behind!

One night I nabbed a couple of seats, and kept one for
my little cutie,
But she got lost among the crowd, and in the darkness
sooty,
A dame in uniform took the seat (she wore the same
hats),
I squeezed her little hand, and found - a
commandment in the WATS.

In a cosy little café she and I meet when we're able,
Pretend we're not together, sitting at the corner table.
I never do enjoy the food, although it's appetising.
In case a senior officer comes and finds us fraternising.

But in the gloaming, now and then, beside the stream we roam,
And talk about our wedding and our charming little home.
There's no one there to see us or remind us of our stations,
Except the old man in the moon - and he don't know the regulations.

****

What a hilarious conclusion to the chapter. However there is more to come. What about those who do not readily come to mind when you think of war, who are these? The following chapter provides some interesting stories.

Chapter 8

The Forgotten

'Gone, but not forgotten by loved ones'

The stories of those on the frontline became well-known, either because of the attention given them by the media or because their daring exploits were told with all the suspense you would find in a good thriller novel in the pubs, alehouses, welfare and miners' clubs, gin houses, housewives' tea parties, or by school children embellishing the daring escapades of their fathers, uncles or members of their family.

What must not be forgotten was the vast numbers who worked tirelessly in the background. Their efforts, although going relatively unobserved, nonetheless accomplished vital work.

Without the efforts of these 'unseen armies' of diligent workforce beavering away, things might have turned out differently.

A nation must be fed and before electric, petrol and diesel engines became the norm, it was the 'black diamond' working in harmony with horses that supplied the energy to get the farm equipment moving. Who could not be impressed by those horses which provided the brawn, those magnificent beasts like the Clydesdales who seemed to treat ploughs as if they were matchsticks. Unseen then were the animals, but slowly and surely they were being replaced.

George Korankye

The war brought about mechanisation and for these beasts of burden the writing was on the wall. William Moore (1934-) remembers as a young lad:

'A highlight to me was awaiting the steam engine drum and pitcher which was brought to the farm annually, to thresh the corn and other nearby farms. As young boys were offered 6d a day to clear the chaff and colder at threshing time. It was a dirty job with some danger, one must add, which today would be totally banned.'

The point is that, without coal, the beginning of mass production to feed an ever growing nation's needs could not have happened, or it may possibly have been drastically delayed. Coal not only powered the farm machines but it 'warmed the cockles of the hearth', in fact the whole house. The arrival of the coalman was an essential part of life.

William Moore goes on:

'In the war years…a coalman named Oscar would call every two weeks. He had to come through the front door of the house to put the coal under the stairs in the cupboard. I was scared out of my wits, as Oscar would put fear into me saying he would put me in a sack and take me away. Another fear was the funeral hearse drawn by horses. The men with black top hats with ribbons walking beside, one would think of these as bogeymen.'

Not to be forgotten of course were the numerous ships ploughing the high seas, whose power also came from coal-fired boilers, carrying much need fuel for the military. These ships became an easy target for the opponent, before the development of radar, sonar and the convoy system which provided a defensive shield. The merchant navy paid a heavy price feeding the nation, bringing crucial provisions to stock its larders and materials to replenish its factories, fuel for all manner of machines which required either diesel or petrol.[106]

A careful appraisal of these unseen and at times unacknowledged masses shows that they accepted their roles without question. Who were these unseen volunteers? They included the coal miners who tunnelled and chiselled the black gold from the bowels of the earth. A number of them gave their lives in the search of this precious commodity, which was needed by the country to power its factories, generate electricity, provide warmth to houses, producing the popular saying which endures into the 21st century: 'keep the home fires burning'.

This invisible army of men, women and children - the school leaving age was 14 - although 'out of sight were not out of mind', showed what can be achieved when it doesn't matter who gets the credit in order to get a job done.

The contribution the Bevin Boys made to the war effort has now been finally acknowledged, when Prime Minister Gordon Brown awarded commemorative medals to a few at Downing Street in March 2008.[107]

---

106 For a fuller description of the Merchant Navy's role in WW2, see The Battle of the Atlantic by Morison, S.E. The Two Ocean War and History of United States Naval Operation in World War II in 15 Volumes. Volume I The Battle of the Atlantic and volume X The Atlantic Battle Won deal with the Battle of the Atlantic

107 Bevin Boys were young men conscripted from all over the UK during WW2 to work in the coalmines due to a shortage of men, who were either drafted or volunteered for the armed forces. It is estimated that over 48,000 were 'recruited' as miners. Boys were not released from the pits until many years after the war.

George Korankye

John Wood-Cowling from Corby relates:

'I was a steelworker and my friend Mick MaGahey[108] who was a miner. He told me this story. One day, Mick was drinking in a bar and his friend came into the bar and handed Mick a brown envelope he had just received. Mick opened it, read it and told him that it was bad news as the poor bloke was now being called up to report for basic Army training.

"Aye I don't fancy it, I've nothing against Hitler!" said his friend.

'Well, Mick came up with a suggestion which would enable him to escape this predicament. He suggested to his friend to go down to the colliery the next day and become a miner, as miners were exempt from the Army. His friend was not very enthusiastic.

"Don't fancy coal," he replied.

"Well," said Mick, "it's up to you, it's coal or bullets!"

'After thinking about Mick's words, the guy reluctantly did his training then went down the mine which, lo and behold, went right out under the North Sea. Now the coalface at the colliery was a considerable distance from the pit bottom. One day while walking to the coalface the gaffer said to the men to have a breather for a few minutes, as he could see they were fair pecked. This friend of Mick's asked how much longer it was to the coalface. The gaffer replied that there was still another twenty minutes to go.

---

108 Michael 'Mick' McGahey (1925–1999) was a Scottish miners' leader who never renounced his working class beliefs. It is said locally that his voice was so rough it could literally raise the dead.

212

"I've had enough of this, I'm going back up top," said Mick's friend.

"Hey! You can't go, we're fighting the Germans," said the Gaffer.

"I'm not surprised," said Mick's friend, "we're stealing their coal.'"

Well, according to John Wood-Cowling, the whole squad burst out in laughter, in fact their laughter may well have travelled all the way to the pit bottom then up to the pit top. Their laughter fairly cheered them up all the way to the coalface.

Some felt slightly dejected and forgotten once again, that their contributions had been largely overlooked. In fact, when you consider all their funny episodes you will soon see that they were quite a witty lot really.

The exploits of George Glover and his family are worthy of note. He was stationed at Plodder Lane and he recollects a particular funny incident. His brother, a 'firer', had been part of the London Manchester express to St Pancras, a 200 mile journey. According to him:

'It was a scorching hot day and, after shovelling to build up his fire for departure, he stepped onto the platform for a breather and was wiping the sweat off his face. He stood at the front of his Patriot (Baby Scot) engine when two servicemen walked up to examine the engine, one a British Merchant Navy Officer and the other an American (one of the first over here after the US entered the war).

'As they looked over the engine the YANK said: "Is that old thing expected to take us to Manchester?" His brother ignored his remarks (thinking of his still to come 200 mile hot slog home).

'But the Yank continued his INSULTS by saying, *"YOU BRITS ARE 100 YEARS BEHIND TIMES AND ARE HEATHENS,"* to which his brother replied, "Does that include ME?" The YANK replied, *"IF THE CAP FITS THEN WEAR IT"*.

'The next moment the British Merchant Naval Officer was picking *HIM* up from the track...the two men then boarded the train after first reporting the incident. On the journey back, the signalmen (en-route) tried to get a *GLIMPSE* of the fireman who had knocked a *YANK* off the platform at London (the BUSH telegraph from signal box to box had been busy).

'On arrival at the shed, the gaffer wanted my brother and his driver to go into his office and to warn them they were required to attend a Court of Inquiry at Derby regarding the assault, at which my brother was fined three days *UNPAID STOPPAGES BECAUSE THE* crime WAS assaulting a guest of this country, but he said that HE (his brother) might have to choose his three days. Because he was in digs at Manchester and hadn't been home for ages, he chose four days home leave.' (Italics and capitals George Glover's.)

Is that not how the Americans have come to be perceived? Whatever was in Britain, the Americans had it bigger, better, faster, sleeker, etc. This attitude did breed animosity at times, but it also provided humorous situations. We have all heard of the famous Chindits. [109]

---

109 The Chindits were a Special Forces unit of the British Indian Army. The recruits were drawn from all sorts. Their territory of operations was primarily Burma and India. Their objective was the sabotaging of Japanese military targets. This involved them working behind enemy lines. Their time line of operations was 1942-1945. Similar organisations were the SAS and SBS.

William J A Winfield, who served primarily in India and Burma in the 14th Army during WW2 and who is sadly now deceased (1979), is reputed to have told his son Peter [110] the following tale:

'Perhaps not so humorous is when he (his father William Winfield) met up with my uncle Bert who had volunteered to be a Chindit. Bert was a regular soldier who volunteered for everything, including parachuting into German-occupied Crete.

'He went on to become the Regimental Sergeant Major of the Queen's Regiment. He liked fighting.

'They were out for a drink one night, off duty, when they came across a fight in a bar between soldiers from a Scottish Regiment and American Airforce personnel. Bert suggested they join in, but my father thought two WO1's should set an example.

'Bert suggested they pull their sleeves down over their WO1 wrist badges, and so they did. Fortunately, they left just before the military police arrived.

'My father said there were many more Americans who had to be helped away than the Scots!'

Talking of Chindits, Noonan[111] relates a story whereby Commander Wingate in an effort to let his men get a realistic appraisal of what they were in for said, 'You are going to die in Burma.'

'In that case,' said the rifleman, 'I'm not bloody well going.'

Then of course there were the prisoners of war (POWs) who suffered tremendously at the hands of the

---

110 Peter Winfield, WW2 The People's War. Courtesy BBC.

[111] *Tales From the Mess* (1983) by Miles Noonan p91.

enemy. The famous film 'The Bridge over the River Kwai' portrayed some of the incidents. [112]

Gail Wesson, a 70-year-old Canadian, was watching the program 'Great Escape - Canadian Story' on the History Channel and saw her Uncle Bruce Baker (Norwood, Ontario Canada) in a photograph at the beginning and end of the film. He was in Stalag Luft3 (Stalag Luft III) during the war.[113]

It appears Bruce Baker was shot down in a Halifax bomber off the coast of Denmark in April 1943. There are lots of stories of the camp, but here is the poem composed by the prisoners of the unit that Gail sent in from Canada to the author.

Stalag Luft III

Here we are at Stalag 3
Drinking at the bar
With lovely girls to buy us beer
Like 'Bloody Hell' we are!

We travelled here in luxury
The whole trip for a quid
A sleeping birth for each of us
Like 'Bloody Hell' we did.

---

[112] The film *The Bridge on the River Kwai* (1957) was based on the fictional novel with a similar title. Both are WW2 dramatisations of the construction the Burma Railway in 1942-43. It showed the appalling loss of life that went into building this railway.

[113] *The Great Escape* (1963) is a WW2 film which, it is said, is actually based on true events. It tells of POWs who, after repeatedly escaping, are put in secure camp Stalag Luft III. However, they still manage to escape from the camp.

Die Laughing – War Humour

Our feather beds are two feet deep,
The carpets almost new,
In easy chairs we sit all day
Like 'Bloody Hell' we do.

The goons are bloody wizard chaps
Their hopes of victory good,
We'd trade them places any day
Like 'Bloody Hell' we would!

When winter comes and snows around
The temperature at nil
We'll find hot-water bottles in our bed,
Like 'Bloody Hell' we will!

It's heaven on earth at Stalag 3,
A life we'd hate to miss,
It's everything we'd always want
Like 'Bloody Hell' it is!

And when this war is over
And Gerry gets his fill
We'll remember all that's here
My 'Bloody Oath' we will!!!

Talking of POWs, the story of Bill's father comes to mind. His father served on *HMS Kepel*, a destroyer in the Royal Navy, from 1939-1945. There is anecdotal evidence the Germans were very meticulous, so precise was their behaviour that at times it could be predicted in advance. One of the main reasons that enabled prisoners to escape from POW camps was simply that prisoners could calculate to a minute when the guards would change, how often they would be inspected and even the number of steps they took coming round the various sheds.

There appears to be an element of truth in this. Bill's father's story provides convincing evidence. He relates:

'My father served in the British navy 1939-1945, the majority of his service on *HMS Kepel* (subject of a famous court case in the 1970s I believe) a destroyer bought from the Canadians at the start of the British conflict. The ship was assigned on this occasion to convoy runs to Russia. The ship was heading up to Bear Island when, like clockwork, the German spotter plane came out to watch which direction the convoy was going, flying round and round in circles above them. The Captain was getting a bit browned off with this so asked his signalman (I think that is what you call him) to "flash" Morse code at the pilot and ask him: "Would you please circle in the opposite direction, as you are making us all really dizzy".

The German pilot signalled back in English: "Anything to oblige" and proceeded to circle in the opposite direction.'

Speaking of Germans, we must not forget their engineering skills. You only have to look at their engineering products to see the proof of this statement. Yes, many will ask immediately, did not Britain produce the Spitfire, the saviour of Britain, which 'whipped' the Messerschmitt in the Battle of Britain? That is true, but credit where it is due.

The Germans were also to build the dreaded V Rockets. Had these innovative weapons not been destroyed who knows what the outcome of the war would have been?

The rest of the world, especially the United States, was to go on to benefit from the rocket science developed by von Braun (Dr Wernher Magnus Maximilian Freiherr 1912-1977) and his compatriots. It is reputed that had the United States not captured Von Braun and his co-associates the space programme may very well not have achieved the success it did in such a short space of time, thus enabling the United States to put a man on the moon.

Ron Goldstein, featured earlier, has another yarn for consideration concerning POWs:

'In June 1945, my Regiment, the 4th Queen's Own Hussars, was running a POW camp for Germans that had surrendered to us at the war's end.

'The entertainment officer had decided that it would be a good idea to open the local gasthaus or pub for our troops, but the proprietor of the said pub had no beer.

'I went with the entertainments officer to the pub to act as interpreter and explained that the publican was suggesting that if the pub was in effect taken over by our regiment then he could get the beer from the local distillery, which was now under the control of AMGOT, or the Allied Military Government.

'Arrangements were made for us to turn up at the pub with a 7 tonner and the pub owner loaned us loads of barrels.

'We were then taken to the right place near Spittal and the manager of the distillery had fresh barrels of beer loaded for us on to our truck.

'We had just finished loading, and the distillery manager was keen to get a signature from us to keep things in order.

'My officer casually said to me: "Sign for it will you while I get my things together".

'I was not completely convinced that what we were doing was completely legal so, when a place in a ledger was presented for my signature, I signed it as TOM MIX (a cowboy hero of my younger days).

'The distillery manager looked over my shoulder and said: "Danke Herr Mix". We beat a hasty retreat and the signature is probably still there today.'

Britain, today, has in some communities become a multicultural society. There are pockets of British who at times it is claimed feel alienated in their own country and within their own communities.

These individuals who find themselves in such a situation must be careful that they do not let the behaviour of a minority automatically make them presuppose that the whole race behaves in that manner.

The story by flying officer Bill Pearson DFC RCAF, whose flying career ended near Koenigsberg toward the end of 1944 when he was taken as a POW, very well illustrates this fact. This is his account:

'Hit by flack knocking out our two port engines, we had been flying low at about 3,500ft, our aircraft was going down fast. I was first out of escape hatch followed by our W/OP L Daniels and then the pilot S/Ldr Sparks.

'I landed heavily on a cobbled road and rolled into a potato garden behind a house and was immediately surrounded and became a POW.

'When I was picked up I was marched to a barn where a dozen or so civilians came to look me over.

'A short time later I was taken by two guards to an open staff car where S/Ldr (squadron leader) Sparks was already seated. The two Luftwaffe officers treated us in accordance with the Geneva Convention.

'We were taken to a Luftwaffe station nearby and searched, possessions removed, i.e. wristwatch, etc, which were placed in a manila envelope and sealed. Believe it or not, I got those things back at the end of the War - forgot how though.'[114]

Did you ever wonder what happened to all the pets during the war, especially when the bombs were falling? We all know the effect Guy Fawkes Night has on pets: they become absolutely demented. The mind boggles about their reactions to explosions and the deafening noises that accompanied these bombings. Trevor Scott, a 27-year-old, remembers a story told to him by his nan:

'...in the car on the way to my sister's 30th birthday the other day. I am heavily into WW2 so I was asking my nan was she living in London at the time or where she is now, which is just outside Slough (England) near Burnham train station? She told me that she used to visit relatives in London during the war and stay up there for a few days.

'One day the siren went off and they were all going over to the shelter. They could see a doodlebug coming along the path of the road.

A friend of the family had a pet duck so, as well as all the people in the shelter, they had to make room for the duck too.

'Not that it's funny, I know, but a nice little story I thought. I think Nan said that they dropped incendiary bombs at that time and everywhere was ablaze when they came out of the shelter.'[115]

---

114 Bill Pearson, WW2 The People's War. Courtesy BBC.
[115] Trevor Scott, WW2 The People's War. Courtesy BBC.

Anyway, it was not only ducks that man saved. Here is a story told by Richard Holloway about the uncanny sense his dog Rusty seemed to have. This certainly was no 'dumb animal':

'This is a tale of Rusty, our Cocker Spaniel. We lived in Bristol during the blitz. Most evenings my father would take Rusty for his last walk of the day at about 9.30pm. But if there was going to be a blitz later that night, Rusty would not go outside the door. As with so much else, we just accepted this at the time.

'It gave us an extra warning, but every night anyway, we all slept in the kitchen, our safest room, with a corrugated iron shelter over the window, a stack of candles and every pan and bucket filled with water. What remarkable sense did Rusty have? Could he hear the throb of the planes on their way?'[116]

A very poignant question and one no doubt will lead to countless debates and discussions in the pubs and at dinner tables. In fact, during the Tsunami of December 2004 it was reported that the animals all seemed to have a terrible foreboding of the impending disaster. Some in zoos were reported as being restless, others in the vicinity of the Tsunami said the animals seemed to instinctively run to higher ground. Many theories have been propagated to explain this phenomenon which animals seem to possess when threatened with disasters.

Len Scott tells this story:

'On 7 September 1940, as we later learned, British bombers carried out the biggest and most successful raid

---

[116] Richard Holloway, WW2 The People's War. Courtesy BBC.

of the war on Berlin. On 8 September the German papers headlined: "Big Attack on London as reprisal".

'It was indeed a big attack - a night attack. Even in Blackfen we could see the strategy. The first bomber wave dropped incendiaries (Id), seemingly targeted on the docklands area. The second wave dropped the heavy stuff into the areas so targeted. We had no hesitation in seeking the dugout: Mr and Mrs Morrish, with whom I was billeted, their child, their dog - and me. Around midnight, Morrish got into the kitchen to make tea, that universal panacea, when he heard knocking at the door. There stood my Danish wife Minna, in her ATS uniform - complete with her little terrier, Ib!

'The shelter now grew very warm. The Morrish dog did not care for Ib and the Morrish child did not care for anybody. After my fear-inspired anger towards Minna had died down, she told me about her journey from Aldershot to Waterloo. She had a grandstand view of the docklands destruction and bombs were falling close to the railway. The train often halted. Lineside workers signalled when the next track-section had been reported clear of damage.

'At almost-empty Waterloo Station, Minna and Ib were ordered into a shelter by Air Raid wardens but she spotted a train which was about to leave, Sidcup-wards and ignored them. This route went even nearer the area of attack and the scene, glimpsed through the edges of the drawn blinds, was terrifying. The south side of the Thames was a mass of flames.

'As she walked Ib from Sidcup Station to Blackfen, shards of shrapnel from the AA batteries rattled on the pavements and another Air Raid warden ordered her into a shelter. "I've got my tin hat," she replied. "Yes - but your dog hasn't!" Persuaded that her billet and shelter were close by, he allowed her to pass. We remained in the shelter until dawn when, at last, the all-clear sounded.'[117]

What country in the whole world where man resides, facing a situation where bombs are being dropped like confetti with flames lighting up the skies and the possibility of being gravely injured by pieces of shrapnel, will think of their dog? In some countries dogs are not treated like humans, rather they are treated as if they are dumb animals. However, in good old blighty, dogs had helmets like humans. Some owners went as far as getting gas masks specifically made for them.

No wonder the Germans were terrified of the British. Was it the Germans who were mad or was it the British? Well, it depends from whose point of view you saw things. Some countries would think you were 'mad as a hatter' if you went all out to provide tin hats for a dog.

Many were well aware of the exploits of the servicemen who served in distant climes, but we must not forget the wives who dutifully followed their husbands on dangerous assignments. To some it must have been a cultural shock. The heat must have been unbearable at times.

However, a completely different set of circumstances must have been the animals, insects and other animate organisms whose home was the territory they found themselves in.

Peter Winfield, as mentioned earlier, recollects a story his father told him. After recollecting some grim happenings during his father's posting in the Far East theatre of war he says nostalgically:

---

[117] Len Scott, WW2 The People's War. Courtesy BBC.

'But not all the stories were grim. For example: He had bought a silk dressing gown for my mother and left it on his bed in his bungalow in Poona, India. But it was destroyed by a party of large ants that marched straight through the bungalow destroying the dressing gown and furniture as they went. A large pit had to be dug and petrol used to kill them.'

Another forgotten crowd were the children who were evacuated from London because of the blitz. The thought of being torn apart from their parents must have been traumatic for many of them. Some probably felt it was just an adventure for them; they could just imagine that they were going to boarding school.

Let us see things from a child's perspective. William Moore, whose village became home to many evacuees, relates how evacuees swelled up from 70 to 100 with, initially, one teacher looking after all the pupils ranging from 8 to 14, the then leaving school age:

'In 1940 evacuees were put in a house with a local family. I remember the boys bringing lard sandwiches for their school lunches (no school meals in these days). There was no electricity. Water was from a nearby well, with a WC at the top of the garden. Rats a-plenty, although cats had now been introduced to help dispose of vermin. One wonders what frightening effect this must have had on London children, who probably had tap water and electricity or gas. Flush WC outside, never vermin.'

Some of William's thoughts may have been correct. These 'poor mites' had left beloved ones at home but what we must not forget was the effects that the nightly bombings would have had on young minds. Coming out of shelters, no one knew what awaited them. Would their house be standing? How about those who maybe could not get to the shelter in time?

The upside of the evacuation was that it spared many of these children from experiencing the grim realities of total warfare. Did any humorous events happen to them?

The Home Guards have already been mentioned. However, it would be fair to say that they too were part of this forgotten army and many laughs came at their expense.

John Wheeler remembers in 1940:[118]

'People were asked to join the Local Defence Volunteers (Home Guard). A pal and I went to the local police sergeant and we were the first two people to enlist that night.

'My mother was worried to death. My friend, Nelson, and I sat on a farm cart with Mr Lloyd and waited for the Germans until daylight. It seems so ridiculous now - what could we have done with a farm cart and no weapons? But that was the spirit at the time.'

Presumably the farm cart was pulled by animals. Now what precisely did they hope to achieve when the Germans arrived? At least in hindsight, John realises how foolish they must have looked. No wonder the Home Guards provided fodder - pardon the pun - for cartoonists.

Nancy Bain, who was 18 at the time, remembers being taken to the beach and told to dig trenches:

118 *Forgotten Voices of the Second World War: a new history of world war two in the words of the men and women who were there* (2005) by Max Arthur, p48. Courtesy Random House Publishing.

'On this whole two-mile stretch of beach we were digging this trench, and it was so obviously hopeless because, with the wind and rain and the high tide, all our work would disappear. But we did it, in this extraordinary way, believing that somehow we were defending the country. That was a futile operation. There was a sergeant or an officer every hundred yards saying, "Keep digging".'

You may wonder where the unions were at the time. If that scenario happened today, there would be hoardes clamouring about the abuse of human rights and the respect of a person's dignity. Imagine making a person dig a hole, knowing full well the tide is going to come in to fill it again.

The causes of war are many and varied. However many believe that Hitler was the primary instigator. In the final chapter, read some hilarious poems about what some feel should happen to him.

Chapter 9

Armistice

'Imagine all the people living life in peace. You may
say I'm a dreamer, but I'm not the only one. I hope
someday you'll join us, and the world will live as one'

John Lennon

The chief cause of the war, many believed, was Hitler
and his party followers. It is no wonder then that there are
many cartoons about him and his henchmen. The men
who were dying in their thousands also blamed him for
their predicament. This feeling comes through in many
ways. Even children got in on the act. During the war
they did not play doctors and nurses or Cowboy/girls and
Indians. No they played at impersonating Hitler!

*" I know what—let's pretend we're
Hitler and go and annoy everybody."*

(Copyright *Punch*)

One poem, *Hitler's Dream*, epitomises the religious thoughts of the day. Many believed that the good go to heaven and the bad to a hell fire. And yet Hitler's crimes were so repulsive that some felt that he should not even be granted a safe haven in a hell fire.

Of course, if we reverse the coin, the Germans saw things differently. They no doubt felt that the British were the aggressors. In fact, before the war many Germans too were sounding a note of caution but their warnings fell on death ears. Hitler's life is a stark reminder of the truthfulness of Abraham Lincoln's (1809-1865) words: 'Nearly all men can stand adversity, but if you want to test a man's character, give him power'.

Here is a poem by Roy Gledhill (1912-2003) courtesy of Mrs P A Clay, his daughter.

Hitler's Dream

Here is a story strange as it may seem
Of Hitler the Nazi and his terrible dream;
Being tired of his Allies, he lay in his bed
And among other things he dreamed he was dead.

He was all straightened out, and lying in state
And his little moustache was frozen with hate;
He wasn't long dead when he found to his cost
His plans and his passports to the next world were lost.

On leaving this world to heaven went straight
And proudly stepped to the golden gate.
Peter looked and spoke in a voice loud and clear,
'On your way Hitler you can't come in here'.

So he turned his heels and away he did go
At the top of his speed to the regions below,
But the Angel was worth his hire.
He rung through to Satan, and gave him the wire.

Satan replied: 'Lads. I'm giving you this warning
We are expecting Hitler this morning,
Now get this straight and get this clear
We're too DAMNED good for that fellow down here'.

Satan, Oh Satan, Herr Hitler replied
I've heard what you said while standing outside
Please give me a corner I've nowhere to go
And Satan replied a thousand times 'NO!'

He kicked Hitler out and vanished in smoke
And just at that moment ADOLPH awoke.
He was lying in bed all covered in sweat,
Shouting Doctor Oh Doctor it is my worst dream yet.

To heaven I don't go, I know damned well
But it's darned hard lines when you're kicked out of HELL.

William Maylam in his diary features a Hitler joke:

'Historians are beginning to agree on who made the greatest mistake in history. They have narrowed down the suspects to two - Hitler's mother or his father.'

There appears to be this recurring theme in many people's thoughts. 'They (Hitler and his henchmen) gave no quarter, so invariably they too deserved none' appears

George Korankye

to be the maxim prevailing at the time. Basically, in the case of Hitler and his cronies what does the evidence point to? Are people right to feel this loathing, this anger towards those whom they rightly feel perpetrated this war? Look at the evidence below.[119]

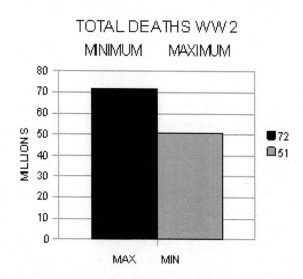

TOTAL DEATHS WW2

The figures are unbelievable. Now imagine driving, no, walking, the length and breadth of Britain from Land's End to John o'Groats and not seeing a single living soul.

Can you see why some devote their whole lives trying to avert it? As one person (Churchill) said, 'jaw-jaw is better than war-war'.

---

[119] Obtaining accurate figures was difficult as different sources quoted varying figures. The author therefore estimated maximum, minimum figures. Full lists of referenced materials are available in the bibliography pages.

In spite of all the aforementioned - and some become justifiably angry - people find humour in such situations.

Mrs S Andrews from Ipswich sent a copy of a relic from her grandfather's scrapbook. According to her:

'He (her grandfather) served in the Royal Artillery in Sierra Leone, discharged in 1912 and in 1914 he volunteered with the 1st Suffolk's to fight on the Somme and Ypres. He survived the war, being discharged on medical grounds.'

Here is a man that served in a battle that experienced one of the worst casualty figures the British have ever experienced. WW1 saw also the introduction of 'gas warfare'.

So bad was it that it was never deployed again by the combatants in WW2 and yet, ironically, during the latter periods of the 20th century it reared its head again, even in the 'enlightened' part of the civilized world.

The release of Agent Orange during the Vietnam War was just another development of this type of warfare.[120]

Anyway, back to Mrs Andrews' heirloom inherited from her grandfather. It contains 'The Kaiser's Last Will and Testament'.

The Kaiser's Despair

Realising that the end is near, he makes his will. From our special correspondent in Berlin.

---

120 Agent Orange was a powerful chemical that stripped vegetation of its foliage. It was used by the United States during the Vietnam War (1959-1975). The dioxins in this chemical concoction have been implicated in many diseases and illnesses. As with the effects of radiation, it has taken time to establish its genetic and long range effects.

It is rumoured in Germany that the Emperor now realises that his number is up, and is accordingly making his Will, revoking all Wills made heretofore. The Will is said to read as follows:

This is the last Will and Testament of me, Wilhelm, the super-swanker and ruler of the sausage-eaters, recognising that I am fairly up against it, and expecting to meet with a violent death at any minute at the hands of brave Johnny Bull, hereby make my last Will and Testament.

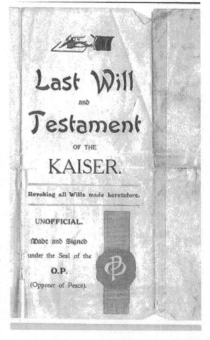

I appoint the Emperor of Austria to be my sole executor (by kind permission of the Allies):

1) I give and bequeath to France the territories of Alsace and Lorraine (as this is only a case of returning stolen property. I don't deserve any credit for it, and am not likely to get it either).

2) To Serbia I give Austria.

3) To Russia I give Turkey, for the Tsar's Christmas Dinner.

4)   To Belgium I should like to give all the thick ears, black eyes and broken noses that she presented me with when I politely trespassed on her territory.

5)   To Admiral Jellicoe I give all my dreadnoughts, submarines, torpedo-boats, destroyers and fleet of funkers generally, what's left of them. He's bound to have them in the end, so this is only anticipating events.

6)   To John Bull I give what's left of my Army, as his General French seems so handy at turning my men into sausage-meat, I suppose he seems to finish the job with his Kitchener, the champion German–sausage cooker.

7)   To the British Museum I leave my famous moustaches, souvenir of the greatest swanker in this or any other age.

8)   To Mrs Pankhurst and the wild women, I leave my mailed fist. They'll find it useful, no doubt, when they resume militant tactics.

9)   To Sir Ernest Shackleton I leave the Pole, I've been up it so long that I regard it as my own property.

Signed: H I M WILHELM,
Lord of the Land, Sea and Air,
Not forgetting the Sausages and Lager Beer

Signed by the above-named WILHELM as his last Will in the presence of us his ministers and keepers present at the same time, who in his presence and in the presence and in the presence of each other have hereunto subscribed our names as witnesses
Baron Von Sauerkraut.
Graf von Munichiagerbier

****

George Korankye

What must not be forgotten were the austere measures put into place to preserve food. Ron, mentioned earlier, recollects:

'During the period October 1945 to January 1947 I was stationed in the Trieste area. The end of the war had seen my unit, the 4th Queen's Own Hussars, change from its wartime footing to its original pre-war role of a prestigious cavalry regiment.

'Fortunately for me I had achieved the lofty rank of corporal and as tech corporal to A Squadron was allowed to get on and do my job without too much parade bashing. Part of the price I paid for this dispensation was being on several committees connected with the welfare of the regiment, one of which was the subtly named "Canteen and Cookhouse Committee" and which included in its ranks the O/Rs Messing Officer.

'We used to meet once a week and had a chance to air our views and make recommendations about future menus. One day someone asked: "What about chips for a change?"

'The Messing officer said, "The only problem is the shortage of frying oil, unless you don't mind the cook using horse fat."

'This immediately produced shrieks of disgust from the committee until the Messing Officer said, "I don't know why you're protesting so much. You've been eating horse for weeks now!"'

The ultimate question of was the war worth all the sacrifices is an interesting one. Many reply 'nay', others 'yea'.

Who is right and what are some of the reasons offered?

Lord William Rees-Mogg in 2004 posed a very interesting question. He asked the pacifists:[121] 'Would you have allowed Hitler to win?' To answer that question he brings the reader to a more modern dictator, that of Saddam Hussein. He, too, was finally toppled. He then goes on to relate the differences between Hitler and Saddam and why they posed different challenges requiring differing solutions.

The conclusion Lord Rees-Mogg reached was that the only way to avoid war situations, he sincerely believed, was for man to change his attitudes towards his fellow man and to stop these aggressive characteristics which appear to dominate the thinking process of many leaders. A kind of rule or ruin doctrine. He says:

'Man, we may concede, is the nastiest of the primates; the most given to murdering his own kind. Man ought to be a co-operative monkey, herbivorous, peaceable and perhaps even monogamous. We could then build the ideal society, the City of God or at least of the Buddha. Such an ideal is to be found in many religions. "The lion shall lie down with the lamb." The trouble is that we do not live in prophetic times. The lion refuses to lie down with the lamb; he seizes the lamb and gobbles him up. We may wish it were otherwise.'

Those thoughts are echoed in the UN statue, which has become such a well-known symbol of peace. This statue was presented by courtesy of the UN at the beginning of this book. It is at the heart of the solution to war. What it is shouting out to us is that war starts with the way humans think. If we do not change our way of thinking we cannot avoid war.

---

121 See 'From Berlin to Fallujah, The Bomb And The Bullet Are An Inevitable Evil' by William Rees-Mogg, *The Times*, 15 November 2004.

The lion lying down with the lamb seems idealistic in the 21st century, but it would appear a solution to be seriously considered. Thousands of years of human rule with its varying methods of rulership have not been able to change man from a lion to a lamb. The question posed at the beginning of this book is worthy of reiteration.

Will man ever be able to fulfil the UN's dream of a peaceful earth? What must not be forgotten was the suffering the 'other side' also experienced. At times, the most forceful way of showing this is to listen to someone who was actually there and hear their experiences.

The poem below by notable war poet Siegfried Sassoon brings home the effect war has on all, whether friend or foe. In fact, a well-known worldly saying is: 'Someone's terrorist is another man's freedom fighter'. Are there any winners in a war? Siegfried Sassoon's poem ensures we think seriously.

Reconciliation by Siegfried Sassoon[122]

When you are standing at your hero's grave,
Or near some homeless village where he died,
Remember, through your heart's rekindling pride,
The German soldiers who were loyal and brave.

Men fought like brutes; and hideous things were done;
And you have nourished hatred, harsh and blind.
But in that Golgotha perhaps you'll find,
The mothers of the men who killed your son.

As was mentioned in Chapter 2, the Germans too could be classed as victims. They marched headlong into

---

[122] © Siegfried Sassoon by kind permission of the Estate of George Sassoon.

a war fuelled by propaganda. Age old rivalries were stimulated by expansionist policies of ambitious men. Some of these soldiers had no option but to enlist in the armed forces. To them, too, it was 'my country right or wrong'.

Therefore, if there is an armistice, if all the wrongs of war have to be forgotten, then it is only fair and proper that the many thousands – no, millions - of German lives lost to all the conflicts should also be remembered.

The Germans have chosen largely to forget their war dead. They have been swept under the carpet, a part of their history they wish had never happened.

Wishing something had never happened does not take away the fact that the incident ever occurred.

Roger Boyer in *The Times* newspaper, 7 June 2008, summaries in a candid way the disrespectful treatment of millions of German war dead who have been left in open fields over the years without a proper burial, with only the growing grass as their covering.

The reason for this is, he says: '...at least part of the blame rests with the Germans themselves who have been ashamed for the best part of half a century about the ordinary German soldier, unsure whether he was a hero or a criminal.'

'In the records of the Wehrmacht, the average Joe tends to exist only in anonymous form, a statistic,' so says the German historian, Dr Wolfram Wette.

The author contacted the German War Graves Commission. Two books were courteously provided. One contained statistical data which the author has permission to reprint.

Would you agree that the Germans, too, paid a heavy price?

George Korankye

Richard Holloway, a child at the time of WW2, tells of his recollections as a boy:[123]

'Part of my school was burnt out by incendiary bombs, resulting in my form being transferred to the hall of a theological college. Sunday afternoons were spent walking to see the anti-aircraft balloon based on the Downs.

'After every blitz I would hunt for "treasures" which were kept in an equally treasured shoe box - pieces of shrapnel, the nosecap of a shell, the tailfin of an incendiary bomb. We all lined up in the avenue to have our gasmasks checked, a hilarious sight, but I felt suffocated and unable to breathe in mine. I remember a train journey from Bristol to Exeter which was so packed with people that I was standing on the moving plates where two carriages joined, with tremendous draughts coming through the joining "concertinas".

'I remember the whole anguish of the blitz, with the city centre destroyed, churches burnt out, houses bombed, businesses lost and overall the anxiety and distress of everyone with relations and friends away fighting or at home in the ARP or fire service and so on. My father had been in the Territorial Army ever since his service in the Great War, hence he was called up when the war started, soon to be invalided out. My brother in the 6th form was on fire watch duties at school. Later he was in the Royal Marines through Holland and Germany. On top of the anxieties this caused, my mother kept those of us at home fed, queuing at the shops with little scope for anything beyond our bare rations. I know now how much she starved herself to keep us fed.

---

123 Richard Holloway, WW2 People's War. Courtesy BBC.

Die Laughing – War Humour

'Although as a child at the time, the war was to me the normality, it has had a profound effect. One hears much of the heroism, comradeship, humour - but this is not war, it is a defence. The real war is horror - uncertainties, nauseating worry, destruction, injury and death. It doesn't just happen in films, or to other people in far off places. It happens to you, to your family, to your life. It left me with a hatred of war!'

Many UK citizens remember the academically acclaimed BBC programme 'The World at War'. This documentary, with excellent photographic footage and eyewitness accounts of WW2, was indeed informative. It helped everyone, from the ordinary 'Joe Bloggs' in the street to the professor of history lecturing at a university, to see in a truthful way the causes of the war through to its final resolution and legacy. The final documentary was simply entitled 'Remember'.

Another question could also be posed, 'Remember' what? The answers may very well be 'Remember' the lessons of war or perhaps even 'Remember' the price paid. As the documentary unfolded, the narrator went through all the various statistics of WW2.

Incidentally, when talking of the final tally of war dead, the number of approximately 50 million as stated by the BBC did not exclude the Germans.[124] All military and civilian deaths were included in this figure.

---

124 The total war dead is only an estimate. Some say the figure is far higher. Nevertheless, we seem not to have learned the lesson. New estimates of total war dead in the second half of the 20th century have been revised from 2 million to proximately 5.4 million. British Medical Journal volume 336, issue 7659, pages 1482-1486. See also Reuters news online at: www.alertnet.org/thenews/newsdesk/N19285476.htm.

Many will say that is bunkum and that the freedoms we enjoy today are only possible because someone was willing to sacrifice their life so that we could all enjoy the freedom of speech we have today.

It is beyond the scope or authority of the author to debate this point. There are people of greater minds and who have far more political 'clout' or influence who have tried to answer this question in various publications.

The point of this book is not to enter into this debate, but to demonstrate that humans have a tremendous capacity for laughter, even when faced with situations that called for fortitude, sacrifices on a scale unparalleled in history. Humans can still have time and energy for a good laugh.

Heather Crook from Preston in a letter written to the author wrote:

'Dear Mr Korankye,

I think you will find the bits I have sent you from my father's memoirs interesting, hope they may be of use to you.

Edwin Preston

'My grandfather was born Edwin Frogette Preston on the 9 November 1891 in Seaforth, Liverpool. He was a builder by trade as was his father. When he went to war he left behind his wife, Teresa, and young daughter, Elsie. When he met his wife she was in service at a big house. They fell in love and she eloped with him one night by climbing down a ladder he brought with him.

'He was an engineer and was often on manoeuvres digging out the trenches and putting up the barbed wire.

'He used to recall that if an officer ordered you over the top you had to go, no two ways about it. On one occasion the Germans had a gun set up and it kept hitting the same place. Men were ordered to go over the top and kept getting shot. My Granddad said. "We can't go up there, it will be certain death to go over." He put his hat on a shovel and knelt against it and wasn't hit, his mate did the same, and luckily neither was hit.

'It amused him that the little Indian children would dive into the water for pennies and even silver paper. He also thought it very strange that, due to lack of water, they often cleaned their pots with sand, but then realised it was like them cleaning their teeth with salt.'

Eric Crook (1917-2007)

'My own father would talk very little about the war. We used to ask him as children, as did grown ups, but he would hardly ever talk about it. Here are some things that I do remember him saying, also excerpts from his memoirs which I am hoping to publish myself soon, but you are welcome to use them. The bits from his memoirs I will put in italics, the rest are just what I remember him telling us.

'He was enlisted towards the end of the war. The farmer he was working for at the time hadn't sent in the necessary papers for him to be excused.'

......everyone thought war, if it came, would be over in six months...The prophets were nearly right, but if the onslaught had only lasted six months, we would have lost and these words would not have been written. In the end we won a war and eventually lost an empire. As it was we bathed in an aura of smug satisfaction, we were

243

unbeatable at anything so why worry. In fact I think the 1938-39 years were the most carefree of our lives.

.....most girls avoided a soldier's company like the plague; 'squaddies' as they were called were strictly taboo, even the lads looked askance and disassociated ourselves from the khaki-clad fellas from Fulwood Barracks.

...not one of us fancied the RAF, well I secretly did, but who wanted to be a Brylcream boy?

Gas masks and identity cards had been issued to all and sundry, earlier on in the year, so everyone became a number without even being in the forces. I was NVTB 241/5 and when hostilities commenced those two items had to be carried at all times. Air raid shelters and emergency water supplies stuck out like sore thumbs and sprung up like a mushroom growth.

Everyone hoped, of course, that it was a case of sabre rattling... Europe was plunged into another maelstrom of deprivation, suffering and witnessed man's inhumanity to man and all the carnage that ensued and bringing in its wake a host of new customs, one which still exists – hitchhiking, thumbing a lift, people with haversacks bulging, expecting one to carry them miles on the cheap. Also squatting, black market, etc and all the Shultz's in the area wondered what recriminations there name would bring.

Women did men's jobs and showed how versatile they could be. Tears flowed when their boys donned the khaki.......

Arthur Eric Crook 1991

******

Last word goes to Mrs Nancy Grove who wrote the letter below. It is another poem about Hitler. This man many believed was responsible for WW2. It is therefore fitting to close this volume with a humorous poem written about him

'Dear Mr Korankye,

'…I hope the enclosed poem will help you. My grandfather wrote it during world war two. He sent it to my uncle who lived in USA. He had it printed and the Scottish Branch of British Red Cross sold it.

'I lived in Glasgow then, as did my grandfather. Every member of our family was given a copy of this poem. I have had mine copied for you.

'I have lived in Bridlington a long time now and when I saw your request thought the poem would be of use to you. The only snag was that it took me until yesterday (3 April 2008)[125] to find it.

'Also I'm sorry I'm not able to e-mail it to you. Hopefully I will hand it into the Free Press tomorrow as they requested.

'Good luck with your book. Let me know if and when it comes out.

Mrs Nancy Grove
PS The war was still going on when he wrote this and he was in his 70s then.'

---

[125] The letter did not reach the author until 17 July 2008 when final draft was at the publisher's copyeditor. The author managed to persuade Mirage Publishing to include this rather humorous poem.

George Korankye

Hitler's Dream

One night a week or two ago
As Hitler lay in bed,
He had a most alarming dream
He thought that he was dead

Towards Heaven he promptly made his way
In hopes to gain admission,
But Peter met him at the gate
And he refused permission.

'Your conduct while on earth' he said,
'Has been so shocking bad,
That if I should allow you in.
They'd say that I was mad.

So go along the other way
And you go straight to.....' well
You know the place that Peter meant
Where wicked sinners dwell.

So Hitler turned with mournful heart
As he was told to go,
And sought a word with him who rules
In regions down below.

His Royal Satanic Majesty
Was sitting on his throne.
When Herr Adolphus Hitler was
Into his presence shown.

'Come forward here,' Old Satan cried,
'Explain your presence here,

Die Laughing – War Humour

I want to hear a true account
Of your wretched vile career'

'Your majesty,' Herr Hitler said,
'On earth I served you well,
As you will quite agree with me
When I my story tell.

The world can vouch that I have sent
Some thousands to their graves,
And any who opposed my will
I made them abject slaves.

I've bombed defenceless fishermen
And as their boats went down,
I laughed with maniacal glee
To see their sailors drown.

And when a group of refugees
From me would try to run,
My brave and gallant soldiers would
Turn on them with their gun.

And Your Gracious Majesty
My deeds are so well known,
I would make a good successor
For your kingdom and your throne.'

'Hold there' growled Satan in a rage,
'You thieving murdering pest,
You'd try to grab my kingdom too
As you've done the rest.

Get out of here you blood stained thief

And quickly turn about'
With that the Imps all gathered round
And boldly kicked him out.

Then Hitler woke up with a start,
His body wet with sweat
He clenched his teeth and muttered low,
'By heck I'll get you yet.

For when I've finished with this war
And laid Great Britain low,
I'll come again with all my men
And bomb you down below.

My undefeated Storm Troops
And gallant Nazi legions
Will force you to capitulate
And leave the Nether Regions'

By D Adams

In the preface, the 'dream' of the UN was epitomised in its iconic statue (see following page). Perhaps a fitting conclusion would be another UN 'dream'.

To reiterate the sentence in the introductory section: 'Will man ever be able to fulfil the UN's dream of a peaceful earth?' or are we for eternity going to say what Aristotle (384-322BC) said in the past: 'We make war that we may live in peace'? Only time will tell!

This sculpture was a gift from the Government of Luxembourg presented to the United Nations in 1988.

It consists of a large replica in bronze of a 45-calibre revolver, the barrel of which is tied into a knot. It was created in 1980 as a peace symbol by artist Karl Fredrik Reutersward.

Die Laughing – War Humour

The sculpture below is located in the Visitor's Plaza, facing First Avenue at 45th Street. © UN images

Bibliography

1915 The Death of Innocence (1993) Lyn MacDonald Headline Book Publishing London

A Basinful Of Fun Back to Civvies No 42 by F Youngman Ltd Leeds

A History of the World 1901 to the Present Twentieth Century (1999) by Roberts The Penguin Press London

Carry On Yomping More Cartoons From 'Up The Falklands' (1982) by Roy Carr, Arthur Huddart and John Webb Blandford Press Dorset

Cheerful Sacrifice The Battle Of Arras 1917 (1990) by Jonathan Nichols Octopus Publishing Group London

Chronicle of the 20th (CD) Century DK Media London

Dictionary of the First World War (2006) by S Pope and E Wheal Pen and Sword Military Books Ltd United Kingdom

Dictionary of the Second World War (2003) by S Pope and E Wheal Pen and Sword Military Books Ltd United Kingdom

Erzählen ist Erinnern Volksbund Deutsche Kriegsgräberfürsorge (1999) by German War Graves Commission

Europe At War (1941) by Low Penguin Books London

Europe Since Versailles (1940) by Low Penguin Books Ltd Londo

Forgotten Voices of The Great War A New History of WW1 In The Words Of The Men And Women Who Were There (2003) by Max Arthur Random House Publishing London

Forgotten Voices of The Second World War A New History of World War Two in the Words Of The Men And Women Who Were There (2005) by Max Arthur Random House Publishing London

Hard Times and Humour Tasburgh 1939-197 (2004) by William Moore L.F Everett and Son Dereham

Hitler's Traitors German Resistance to the Nazis (2003) by Susan Ottaway Leo Cooper Publishers London

http://en.wikipedia.org/wiki/Encyclopedia in formation retrieved August 2008

I Couldn't Help Laughing an Anthology of Wartime Humour (1941) Edited D.B Wyndham Lewis Lindsay Drummond Ltd. London

Last Post The Final Word From Our First World War Soldiers (2005) by Max Arthur Orion Publishing London

Laugh While You Work More New Cartoons and Jokes by Jay Publications London

Laughingitoff Sixth Spasm You'll Be Tickled To Death by Gerald Swan Ltd London

Lest We Forget Forgotten Voices From 1914-1945 (2007) by Max Arthur Random House Publishing London

More Tales From The Mess A Further Military Miscellany (1985) by Miles Noonan Arrow Books Ltd London

Mr Punch's History of The Great War (1919) by Cassell and Company Ltd London

Occupied England A Selection of Drawings and Jokes by Pictorial Art Ltd London

Over The Top (1983) by Roy Carr, Arthur Huddart and John Webb Blandford Press Dorset

Poets of the Great War (1999) by T. Holt, V Holt and C Zeepvat Pen and Sword Military Books Ltd United Kingdom

Salute The Soldier (1966) Edited by Captain Eric Bush George Allen And Unwin Ltd London

Schicksal in Zahlen Volksbund Deutsche Kriegsgräberfürsorge e.V. (2000) by German War Graves Commission

Stand By Your Beds Memories of National Service in the Royal Air Force 1947 to 1962 (1995) by John Hamlin GMS Enterprises Peterborough

State Secrets Behind the Scenes of the 2Oth Century (2006) by National Archives London

Still More Bystander Fragments from France No 3 by Bruce Bairnsfather The Bystander London

Bibliography

Suffering From Cheerfulness The Best Bits From The Wipers Times (2007) by Ian Hislop Little Books Ltd London

Tales From The Mess A Military Miscellany (1984) by Miles Noonan Arrow Books Ltd London

The Daily Graphic Special War Cartoons No 4 by H.R Baines and Co Ltd London

The Daily Graphic Special War Cartoons No 5 by H.R Baines and Co Ltd London

The First Day on the Somme (2006) by Martin Middlebrook Pen and Sword Military Books Ltd United Kingdom

The Gutenberg Project (2008) retrieved July 2008 http://www.gutenberg.org/wiki/Gutenberg

The Oxford History of the Twentieth Century (1998) Edited by Michael Howard and Roger Louis Oxford University Press Company United Kingdom

The Quiet Heroes British Merchant Seamen at War (2002) by Bernard Edwards Pen and Sword Military Books Ltd United Kingdom

The Philosophy of Conflict, and Other Essays in War-Time (1919) by Havelock Ellis Ayer Publishing

The Two Types by Jon British Army Newspaper Unit

The Women's Century (2006) by Mary Turner National Archives London

They Make Us Smile (1942) by Percy Bradshaw The Sun Engraving Company Ltd London

Time Almanac of the 20th Century (CD) Softkey International London

Tommy The British Soldier On The Western Front 1914-1918 (2004) BY Richard Holmes Harper Collins Publishing Ltd London

Up The Falklands Cartoons From The Royal Marine (1982) by Roy Carr, Arthur Huddart and John Webb Blandford Press Dorset

What A war by Gilbert Wilkinson Odhams Press Ltd London

Women at War (2002) Edited by Nigel Fountain Imperial War Museum London

George Korankye

World War 11 In Cartoons (1989) by Mark Bryant Grubb Street Publishing London

WW2 The People's War (2008) retrieved July 2008 bbc.co.uk/ww2peopleswar

Your Country Needs You Expansion of the British Army Infantry Division 1914-1918 (1999) by Martin Middlebrook Pen and Sword Military Books Ltd United Kingdom

Other Titles

A Prescription from The Love Doctor: How to find Love in 7 Easy Steps - Dr Joanne 'The Love Doctor' Coyle
Burnt: One Man's Inspiring Story of Survival - Ian Colquhoun
Cosmic Ordering Guide - Stephen Richards
Cosmic Ordering Connection - Stephen Richards
Cosmic Ordering: Chakra Clearing - Stephen Richards
Cosmic Ordering: Oracle Healing Cards – Stephen Richards
Cosmic Ordering: Oracle Wish Cards – Stephen Richards & Karen Whitelaw Smith
Cosmic Ordering: Rapid Chakra Clearing – Stephen Richards
Life Without Lottie: How I survived my Daughter's Gap Year - Fiona Fridd
Internet Dating King's Diaries: Life, Dating and Love – Clive Worth
Mrs Dalrey's Pagan Whispers: A Celebration of Pagan Festivals, Sacred Days, Spirituality and Traditions of the Year – Carole Carlton
Past Life Tourism - Barbara Ford-Hammond
Rebel Diet™: They Don't Want You To Have It! – Emma James
The Butterfly Experience: Inspiration For Change - Karen Whitelaw Smith
The Hell of Allegiance: My Living Nightmare of being Gang Raped and Held for Ten days by the British Army – Charmaine Maeer with Stephen Richards

The Real Office: An Uncharacteristic Gesture of Magnanimity by Management Supremo Hilary Wilson-Savage - Hilary Wilson-Savage
The Tumbler: Kassa (Košice) – Auschwitz – Sweden - Israel - Azriel Feuerstein (Holocaust survivor)

Mirage Publishing Website:

www.miragepublishing.com

Submissions of Mind, Body & Spirit, Self Improvement, How To, Biography and Autobiography manuscripts welcomed from new authors.